"Finally, a workbook that goes right to the beating heart of anxiety: uncertainty. Teens will be guided, step by step, toward increasing awareness, acceptance, and willingness in the face of the vast variety of uncertain situations they may face. A unique and important contribution to the field and a must-read for teens, parents, and therapists alike."

—**Chris McCurry, PhD,** author of *Parenting Your Anxious
Child with Mindfulness and Acceptance,* and coauthor of
The Mindfulness and Acceptance Workbook for Teen Anxiety

"*Getting Comfortable with Uncertainty for Teens* is a gift to every stressed and anxious teen. The authors offer ten powerful tips to help teens understand, tolerate, and ultimately master the uncertainty that is both a source of suffering and the juice of life. I highly recommend it."

—**Michael A. Tompkins, PhD, ABPP,** codirector of the
San Francisco Bay Area Center for Cognitive Therapy,
and author of *The Anxiety and Depression Workbook for Teens*

"This book draws on acceptance and commitment therapy (ACT) principles, and presents a range of evidenced-based ideas in a way that does not talk down to the reader. Teens will learn how to connect to the present, treat themselves with more compassion, identify their values, and plan how to take steps toward these. With such a range of helpful tips, there's likely to be something helpful for every teen struggling with anxiety."

—**Ben Sedley,** psychologist, author of *Stuff Th*
and coauthor of *Stuff That's Loud*

"Negreiros and Martinez have written a clear and practical guide to help young people navigate fear and worry associated with the uncertainties of our modern society. The authors demonstrate an empathetic connection with today's youth, and use their many years of experience to provide a comprehensive tool kit that will help all young people come to terms with the threat of uncertainty."

—**Ronald M. Rapee, PhD,** distinguished professor and director of the Centre for Emotional Health at Macquarie University, and author of *Helping Your Anxious Child*

"*Getting Comfortable with Uncertainty for Teens* addresses a very common struggle, seamlessly blending cognitive behavioral therapy (CBT) and ACT to create a much-needed resource for teens. It provides powerful life skills for accepting and embracing uncertainty, pursuing passions, and cultivating self-compassion. The exercises can be done anywhere, anytime, and the short quizzes are super helpful for increasing self-insight into one's behavior and willingness to implement new strategies. I greatly enjoyed reading this book and highly recommend it."

—**Tamar D. Black, PhD,** educational and developmental psychologist, and author of *ACT for Treating Children*

"In this book, Negreiros and Martinez do an excellent job of introducing the reader to the role that uncertainty plays in worry and anxiety, and they do so in a friendly and approachable manner. This book is chock-full of practical tips and strategies for inviting uncertainty into one's life, and becoming a more confident, social, and happier person as a result. This book will be an invaluable resource for any teen struggling with worries in daily life."

—**Melisa Robichaud, PhD,** coauthor of *The Generalized Anxiety Disorder Workbook* and *The Worry Workbook*

"The formidable duo of Negreiros and Martinez have created what will surely become a leading self-help book for teens living with disabling fear, anxiety, and worry. Drawing upon research and decades of clinical experience with youth, they provide a straightforward guide via teen-friendly, accessible language. What makes this book stand out is the attention paid to promoting evidence-based approaches while concurrently offering practical tips and pearls of wisdom. In summary, I am *certain* that this book will enormously and positively impact the lives of youth who follow the ten described steps towards embracing uncertainty!"

—**S. Evelyn Stewart, MD,** professor of psychiatry at the
University of British Columbia, and coauthor of *OCD in
Children and Adolescents*

"As a parent of teens and a mental health advocate, it is a pleasure and relief to read a book about uncertainty and anxiety that empowers teens in a challenging, validating, and engaging way. I like that the book is structured and includes practical knowledge and skill building activities such as quizzes and takeaways. And even better that these tips are written by trusted experts who treat teens every day."

—**Judith Law,** CEO of Anxiety Canada, a Canadian charity
dedicated to reducing the barrier of anxiety so people can
live the life they want

the *instant* help
solutions series

Young people today need mental health resources more than ever. That's why New Harbinger created the **Instant Help Solutions Series** especially for teens. Written by leading psychologists, physicians, and professionals, these evidence-based self-help books offer practical tips and strategies for dealing with a variety of mental health issues and life challenges teens face, such as depression, anxiety, bullying, eating disorders, trauma, and self-esteem problems.

Studies have shown that young people who learn healthy coping skills early on are better able to navigate problems later in life. Engaging and easy-to-use, these books provide teens with the tools they need to thrive—at home, at school, and on into adulthood.

This series is part of the **New Harbinger Instant Help Books** imprint, founded by renowned child psychologist Lawrence Shapiro. For a complete list of books in this series, visit newharbinger.com.

getting comfortable with **uncertainty** for **teens**

10 tips to **overcome** anxiety, fear & **worry**

JULIANA NEGREIROS, PhD
KATHERINE MARTINEZ, PsyD

Instant Help Books
An Imprint of New Harbinger Publications, Inc.

INSTANT HELP, the Clock Logo, and NEW HARBINGER are trademarks of New Harbinger Publications, Inc.

Distributed in Canada by Raincoast Books

Copyright © 2022 by Juliana Negreiros and Katherine Martinez
    Instant Help Books
    An imprint of New Harbinger Publications, Inc.
    5674 Shattuck Avenue
    Oakland, CA 94609
    www.newharbinger.com

Cover design by Amy Shoup; Acquired by Elizabeth Hollis Hansen; Edited by Karen Schader

Library of Congress Cataloging-in-Publication Data

Names: Negreiros, Juliana, author. | Martinez, Katherine A., author.
Title: Getting comfortable with uncertainty for teens : 10 tips to overcome anxiety, fear, and worry / Juliana Negreiros and Katherine Martinez.
Description: Oakland, CA : Instant Help Books, New Harbinger Publications, [2022] | Series: Instant help solutions series | Includes bibliographical references. | Audience: Ages 13-19 | Audience: Grades 7-9
Identifiers: LCCN 2021052632 | ISBN 9781684039371 (trade paperback)
Subjects: LCSH: Uncertainty--Juvenile literature. | Anxiety in adolescence--Juvenile literature. | Worry in adolescence--Juvenile literature.
Classification: LCC BF463.U5 N44 2022 | DDC 155.5/1246--dc23/eng/20211104
LC record available at https://lccn.loc.gov/2021052632

Printed in the United States of America

24   23   22

10   9   8   7   6   5   4   3   2   1   First Printing

Contents

Introduction

Welcome to *Getting Comfortable with Uncertainty for Teens!* This guide will take you on a ten-tip journey on how to deal with the uncertainty in everyday situations and manage unwanted worry, stress, and anxiety. By knowing how uncertainty affects your life and what to do to cope with overwhelming thoughts and feelings, you may find it easier to pursue your passions and live a life filled with fun, challenges, and achievements.

Uncertainty is one of the roots of human suffering. We all experience different degrees of it. Some people can leave uncertainty in the background and continue to do things that are important or matter to them. Others have a harder time moving forward when they are hit by the harsh reality of facing the unknown. If you find yourself struggling with anxiety and stress that stem from uncertainty and would like to have tools to deal with this, this book is meant for you. *Getting Comfortable with Uncertainty for Teens* is intended to help you in different ways:

- It will help you better handle uncertain situations that generate unwanted stress, worry, or anxiety.

- It will help you identify when uncertainty is taking you down a path that does not align with your passions and life pursuits.

- It will improve your experience and enjoyment in different areas of life, including relationships; school and work; leisure activities; and personal growth, health, and wellness.

Another important potential outcome of this book is that you may change your relationship with uncertainty. Instead of struggling with it, you will find that uncertain situations and their associated feelings and thoughts become opportunities to practice flexibility and develop new ways of coping. As a result, the more you learn to tolerate and cope with uncertainty, the stronger you become in managing all forms of stress and anxiety.

We strongly encourage you to pace yourself while reading the tips as there are lots and lots of skills to learn that need practice and repetition to work. We suggest you take about one to two weeks to read through and implement the exercises of each tip. That way, your brain will have enough time to process and remember the information when you need it the most.

Please note that this guide is not a book on strategies to avoid uncertainty. In fact, you will learn that the more you try to escape uncertainty, the worse life gets in the long run. The reality is that when you realize uncertainty is not your enemy and start making room for it, stress and anxiety will gradually become background noise and take the passenger's seat, leaving you with more energy and time to devote to fun and meaningful interactions and activities. We hope you find guidance and inspiration from the activities and stories we'll share throughout this book and discover that uncertainty can be a source of strength rather than weakness.

A Final Note: Welcome! We are so pleased you have decided to pick up this book and wanted to share a bit of ourselves before we embark. We are both registered psychologists who work with children, teens, and young adults who struggle with anxiety and other related conditions. We are also cis-gender, white, straight, agnostic (neither believe nor disbelieve in a god or religious doctrine), non-disabled females born and raised in other countries (Juliana in Brazil and Katherine in the United Kingdom). Our life experiences have shaped our perspectives, and we acknowledge that we also hold some unearned privilege. However, even if our histories or worldviews differ from our clients, we strive to understand and help them recognize how their unique experiences shape who they are and see these as a blessing. We have our clients to thank for the narratives described in each Tip, as these are a blend of the stories shared with us. Even if these narratives do not represent your experience, we hope you can still appreciate what it might feel like to walk in that person's steps. You may also choose to mentally modify the narrative to align better with your experience and help you get the most out of each Tip. We wish you an insightful and smooth journey as you proceed and learn how to be comfortable with uncertainty!

Becoming Aware: Understanding Uncertainty

This chapter's mission is to help you become an expert on understanding and being aware of uncertainty and how it affects you. How knowledgeable and aware are you about the effects of uncertainty?

1	2	3	4	5
not much		*some*		*a lot*

Wouldn't it be nice to know how life is going to go? Just imagine you have a time machine to the future, and the ride is free. You can time travel and find out whether your teacher will like your project, the sleepover or party will be amazing, or your crush will text you! Maybe you'd love a glimpse into the far future just to be sure that you get into the college of your dreams and live in a cool place, or that the crushing debt your family has will be solved by your hard work and financial success.

Even if the outcomes aren't what we want, most of us would still like to know, at least some of the time, what's going to happen. We call this need to know *certainty,* and given the choice, most of us want it. But alas, there is no time machine to the future. And as a result, for some of us, the not knowing, or the *uncertainty,* makes us feel uncomfortable, affecting our thoughts, feelings, physical sensations, and actions.

WHAT IS UNCERTAINTY?

To begin meeting this tip's mission, we need to start by understanding what uncertainty is and why some people really don't like it. Uncertainty arises when we don't know what lies ahead. Uncertain = unknown, and more specifically, the negative unknown. Uncertainty can be defined as a fear of undesirable outcomes arising from the potential unknowns and an inability to accept that an adverse or bad event might occur, whether or not it's likely to happen. People don't usually equate positive unknowns with uncertainty, but rather with excitement. For example, looking forward to a fun trip or vacation, wondering if you'll get asked to prom, or awaiting a favorite show's new season generally causes excitement, not discomfort.

In contrast, uncertainty is the fusion of moderate to high levels of anxiety about potential negative outcomes, coupled with a dose of discomfort, and the perception that one cannot cope well with what might happen. It is understandably a state some people fear and are intolerant of because it often feels unbearable, affecting what we think, feel, and do when faced with it. But why is this? Where does this fear come from? (Carleton 2016; Carleton, Norton, and Asmundson 2007; Grupe and Nitschke 2013)

WHY HUMANS LIKE CERTAINTY

Human beings like certainty. This liking stems from our ancient ancestors who needed to survive alongside saber-toothed tigers and poisonous berries. Our brains evolved to help us attend to threats, steer clear of them, and remain alive afterward. In fact, we learned that the more certain we were about something, the better chance we had of making the right choice. Is this berry the same shape as last time? The same size? If I know for certain it is, my brain will direct me to eat it because I know it's safe. And if I'm uncertain, my brain will send out a danger alert to protect me. The dependence on certainty all those millennia ago ensured our survival to the present day, and the danger-alert system continues to protect us. This is achieved by our brains labeling new, vague, or unpredictable everyday events and experiences as uncertain. Our brains then generate sensations, thoughts, and action plans to keep us safe from the uncertain element, and we live to see another day.

But for some of us, the danger-alert sensations, thoughts, and action plans get fused with anxiety and fear through a process called classical conditioning (when a neutral item gets paired with an unpleasant item), and even after the potential threat has passed (for example, the new substitute teacher turns out to be okay), those anxious sensations, thoughts, and actions persist (for example, continuing to worry about substitute teachers all year long whether you have any or not). Over time and with repeated experiences, the person's brain becomes primed to expect the worst every time it encounters new, vague, or unpredictable events and experiences, resulting in the person being fearful and intolerant of the unknown.

So, if you're someone who worries, panics, or gets easily stressed out when faced with uncertain situations, then a fear of the unknown is probably at the heart of it all. The less we know, the more we worry.

As certainty ↑, our worry about negative future events ↓

And this stems from the experiences of our ancient ancestors. So now that you know what uncertainty is and why we don't like it, your awareness is on the rise. However, another question remains: why do some of us struggle more with uncertainty than others?

THE UNCERTAINTY STRUGGLE

If you're like many of the teen clients we work with, you may have been struggling with worry, fear, and anxiety for a while now, and underneath this struggle lies an intolerance of uncertainty. But why is this your experience and not everyone's? Why isn't your neighbor or best friend just as gripped by fear and uncertainty as you are when a pop quiz is announced or you're waiting for a decision about the job you applied for? The answer is a bit more complex than you may think. Even scientists don't have all the answers yet and are hard at work trying to unravel this mystery. But so far, there are two contenders to explain why we aren't all equally afraid and intolerant of uncertainty: (1) our uniqueness and (2) allergies!

Unique You

Each of us is who we are because of a mix of the genetic material we're born with, such as whether we have a family history of anxiety or other mental health conditions (adolescents who have a family member, or members, with a mental health condition have a higher chance of struggling with anxiety and uncertainty themselves), as well as our temperament or personality style, and our environment. Some kids are more cautious and reserved than others because of their genes and begin life that way long before experiences have a chance to shape their behaviors. These kids tend to be more anxious and, at times, perceived as shy, compared to other kids.

All of this then interacts with the type of environment we live in. Environmental influences include how we have been raised, our relationships, exposure to hardship and trauma, and availability of resources. For example, some parents are overly controlling, which can contribute to their children being less able to solve their own problems or cope with routine challenges. As a result, these kids may have increased anxiety when faced with uncertainty. In addition, teens who have experienced extreme hardship, such as poverty, abuse or oppression, family discord, or trauma, are more likely to be anxious. And finally, when youth live in enriched and supportive environments that validate their experiences and nurture their needs, for obvious reasons, they are less likely to struggle with anxiety and fear of uncertainty.

In summary, there are literally millions of possible combinations of influences that result in who we are, including whether we become someone who is anxious and fearful of uncertainty. Fortunately, it's a well-supported fact that biology and early life experiences are not destiny. So, if you are someone with a genetic and environmental history that increases your chances of being anxious and struggling with uncertainty, there are still lots of things you can do to help change the way you respond to uncertainty. Through learning skills and finding support, you can learn to become less anxious over time.

The Uncertainty Allergy

Being aware that you are unique and that millions of factors have contributed to who you are, and how anxiety and uncertainty affect you, is only one part of the puzzle. There's something else that can also help answer this interesting question: why are some people more intolerant of anxiety and uncertainty than others? After all, although genetics and environmental experiences have shaped who you are, you've likely tried a bunch of ideas to decrease or even eliminate anxious thoughts and feelings. In fact, you may have worked very hard using lots of skills that smart people have told you should work. Still, despite your efforts, these anxious thoughts and feelings keep returning, and your difficulty tolerating uncertainty persists. It turns out there is a reason for this: you're allergic to uncertainty!

Some researchers in Quebec came up with the clever idea that how a person copes with uncertainty can be compared to how an allergic person copes with an allergen (Robichaud, Koerner, and Dugas 2019). If you're allergic to pollen, even a small amount of it can cause a big reaction, so people try to avoid their allergens as much as possible to prevent physical discomfort or life-threatening symptoms.

Tolerating uncertainty is like being allergic to pollen. When faced with the unknown, some people experience big reactions such as anxiety, physical stress, and worry. And just like an allergy to pollen, being "allergic" to uncertainty results in the person trying to avoid it at all costs. However, avoidance isn't the most effective solution, whether you are allergic to pollen or uncertainty. This is good because it's almost impossible to avoid pollen on a spring day or to ensure certainty all the time. Ironically, the cause of the allergy is also the treatment! To build up immunity or become inoculated against certain environmental allergens such as pollen, medical professionals give the person small doses of their allergen over time until their body develops enough tolerance of the allergen to no longer be allergic (Bachmann et al. 2020). And this is what the Quebec researchers also discovered. When they exposed people with an allergy to uncertain situations, little by little, those people developed tolerance to the unknown until they could cope well with routine uncertainty. We'll explore this more in Tip 8, but for now, we want you to be aware that a second factor—having an allergy to uncertainty—may contribute to understanding why your difficulty tolerating it persists.

REALITY CHECK

So far in this tip, you've become aware of some important information about uncertainty and our relationship with it. We know that life is very different now than it was when saber-toothed tigers roamed the earth. Most of us don't actually face imminent death on a daily basis anymore. Although we evolved to need certainty once upon a time, certainty isn't critical for our survival in modern times. However, we still rely on the danger-alert system to warn us about threats or to prepare us for important things. For example, getting that pit-in-your-stomach feeling or that rush of adrenaline can be a lifesaver (literally!) if you come across a bear or speeding car, or suddenly remember the test is tomorrow.

So, while we need to be alert to physical danger or important things as they arise, we don't require constant certainty. But our brains haven't caught up to this fact, and while we no longer *need* certainty, we still want it. And when we don't get it, some of us, thanks to our genes and the environment we live in, feel uncomfortable, worried, and stressed. Which brings us to our next set of information about how uncertainty can affect some of us.

Over the past fifteen years, researchers have learned more and more about the effects of uncertainty. Their findings suggest the impact of uncertainty on our daily lives is far-reaching (Carleton 2016; Carleton, Norton, and Asmundson 2007; Fergus and Carleton 2015; Grupe and Nitschke 2013). Specifically, when people struggle to tolerate or cope with uncertainty, they are also more likely to:

- be overly attentive to potential threats and see threats everywhere;

- misinterpret neutral information as negative;

- remember threatening events more readily than nonthreatening events;

- experience increased physiological stress symptoms like elevated heart rate and blood pressure, chest pain, trouble breathing, and insomnia;

- have difficulty with routine problem solving;

- avoid new or ambiguous situations and miss out on important life events;

- struggle with decision paralysis or inaction, feeling like they are stuck;

- experience a host of unpleasant emotions such as worry, anxiety, sadness, frustration, and a sense of unfairness.

Have you encountered any of these experiences? If you have, you're probably struggling with uncertainty to some degree. And as your awareness about this struggle increases, you may be starting to feel—well, anxious—about these negative facts. Fortunately, there is some good news. Just because things have been going one way doesn't mean you can't turn things around or change direction. In fact, the very point of this book is to share scientifically supported information and strategies that can help you figure out whether you really need certainty or if it might be time to gently let it go. And if you find the courage to change your relationship with uncertainty, we have nine more tips to help you put those good intentions into action!

Let's go back to that idea of a time machine to the future. What would happen if it really existed? Would you want to take a ride? Would you really want complete certainty about everything? Ravinder thought it was what she wanted, but then changed her mind.

Meet Ravinder

I'm Ravinder (she/her). I'm in tenth grade in a large urban high school. I've got two younger sisters, and my parents own a small business. My grandma lives with us and helps out a lot, but her sister has just been diagnosed with cancer, and my grandma might have to move in with her to help. We don't know what's going to happen, but I really need to know because my life will change if she moves out. She does so much, like getting my sisters from school, cooking our dinners, and helping me with my homework. It's gonna be up to me to take on those tasks if she leaves, and I need to prepare for that. It'll mean I'll have to drop cross-country and track and quit my job babysitting. Even though my parents won't let me date, I like to hang out with my friends, and I won't have time to do that anymore.

Just thinking about how much my life would change causes me so much anxiety and makes it hard to breathe. I keep thinking that I'll never figure out how to cope, and it feels so unfair. I just want to know what's gonna happen! And yet, in my calm moments, I kinda like not knowing about the future and daydreaming about the longer-term possibilities. The uncertainty of my future means I can pretend anything can happen. Like maybe I'll win a scholarship to college or become a famous architect or develop an important vaccine, and perhaps Grandma will live with us until I have kids of my own! I feel stuck between wanting certainty about what's gonna happen to my grandma, but I'm enjoying the uncertainty of my future and imagining all kinds of exciting possibilities.

UNCERTAINTY: CENTER STAGE IN A TEEN'S LIFE

We've established that most humans like certainty, and there's an evolutionary reason for this. And if you're like lots of other teens (and adults too!), you may feel anxious, stressed, and worried when you don't have certainty. But there is a strange twist, or irony, about being a teenager, which brings us to the last area of awareness we'd like to highlight in this tip: *although you may want certainty, adolescence is one of the most uncertain times in the human lifespan, giving you ample opportunity to get good at coping with it* (except for being a baby or toddler, and who can remember those years anyway?!). Ask any grown-up over the age of thirty how much change they see in a year, and you'll be surprised that it's not that much. Within a single year, most grown-ups can be certain about a whole bunch of things: they'll stay in the same job, live in the same home, date (or stay married to) the same person, have the same friends, go to the same events, and do the same activities. In fact, almost everything about their lives is pretty certain and stable. Of course, big things are uncertain, like how the economy will do, who will win an election, whether there will be a pandemic, and more, but the routine things are pretty certain.

Now think about your life within a single year. Is it certain and stable? Can you rely on everyday life being a sure thing? Although we authors don't know what your daily life contains, we suspect if you're like most of our teen clients, there are a bunch of events and experiences that might be unexpected or uncertain from week to week. Thinking about a one-year span, have any of the following happened, or do you predict they will happen?

Relationships

- Making new friends with someone in a class, club, team, job, etc.

- Having a big change in an important friendship (closer, further apart)

- Starting or ending a romantic relationship

- Having a new teacher, coach, or boss

- Getting into a major fight with a family member or friend

School or work

- Starting a new school

- Having new classes

- Starting a new job or volunteer position

- Failing a quiz or test you expected to pass, or passing when you expected to fail

- Missing an assignment or handing it in late

- Doing better or worse than expected on a report card

- Being honored or disciplined in some way you weren't expecting

Personal growth, health, and wellness

- Making a committed change to improve your health (for example, exercise more, eat healthier, sleep earlier, or reduce electronics use)

- Seeing a therapist

- Noticing body changes

- Taking time to chill and relax regularly

Leisure and recreation activities

- Starting a new hobby or activity for fun

- Learning a new skill (for example, driving, cooking, or playing an instrument)

- Trying or going to a new local hangout place

- Participating in a new sport, club, or organization

Perhaps, for you, there are more changes and unknowns in your everyday life than you first realized. However, for others, things might be steady and certain now, but the immediate future is completely unknown and holds all the uncertainty. Rapidly evolving friendships; attending new classes or sports teams each term or year; going through the changes of puberty; or learning to drive, cook, or hold a job are situations that all require you to experience uncertainty. And not just once or twice, but repeatedly. So, with all this demand to cope with change and uncertainty, do you really want to keep fighting against it? We'll discuss this more in Tips 2, 3, and 4, but consider this a sneak peek at thinking about whether you really want to keep struggling against uncertainty, especially as it comes up a lot during the adolescent years. Wouldn't it be nice to learn to coexist with the unknown? To stop living in the constant state of stress, worry, fear, and anxiety that arises with the pressure to gain certainty?

RECONSIDERING HOW MUCH WE NEED CERTAINTY

Hopefully, you're starting to ask yourself if you really need as much certainty as you first thought. (Hint: saber-toothed tigers are extinct.) Maybe you're also wondering whether you might be better able to cope with uncertainty than you realized. Now may be a good time to reconsider your relationship with uncertainty and open yourself up to the idea that you might be well-positioned to tolerate uncertainty simply because it comes with the territory of being a teen in the twenty-first century. Furthermore, you've become aware that just because you struggle with anxiety and uncertainty doesn't mean you're doomed.

There is a lot you can learn and do to change your relationship with uncertainty. And by reading this book, you'll gain strategies to strengthen your tolerance for uncertainty just like you might strengthen your muscles by going to the gym. Believe it or not, the strengthen-your-brain-muscle analogy is accurate! Brain imaging technology has enabled scientists to demonstrate how the brain can change by using some of the very same strategies outlined in the tips in this book. Knowing this, it's reasonable to conclude that by using these strategies you can get better at rolling with life's many unknowns and spend less energy and time worrying and stressing out. As a result, you may gain some spare time to do what truly matters to you. So, before we move on, let's figure out just how much certainty you like and, therefore, how much hard work we have ahead of us!

QUIZ

Grab some paper and a pen or use your device to record your answers. Choose the option that best reflects how you would handle each situation, even if the situation has not occurred to you or isn't exactly what you have experienced:

1. When I open my eyes in the morning,

    A. I love to know exactly what the day will look like, mapping out my schedule hour by hour, and feeling ready for everything.

    B. I think about what I have to do, but feel okay if my schedule changes as the day unfolds because I don't have to know the precise order of events.

    C. I prefer to keep all options open, not having a plan and letting the day evolve naturally.

2. I post a reply stating my opinion to a group chat and immediately regret sending it when no one responds for several minutes.

    A. I find sitting with the discomfort of not knowing why no one has replied is almost unbearable. I really need someone to write something now! I feel insecure, and I think about deleting the post so my opinion isn't criticized.

    B. I wonder why no one has replied. Maybe they disagree with me? I think of different ways to respond, but feel okay that it'll get sorted out.

    C. I move on to something else to pass the time. I figure other people are also doing a bunch of stuff while we're texting, and they'll post something eventually. Even if they don't agree with my opinion, it's okay. I love debates.

3. When I'm waiting for my grade on a quiz or test…

    A. It's the worst! It's on my mind constantly and I feel like I'll burst out of my skin if I don't find out soon. I sleep badly and I'm grumpy the next day.

    B. It bugs me, and I want to know how I did, but I can hang in there. No news is good news, right?! It's a little hard to fall asleep, but I do.

    C. Tests and quizzes don't bother me because there's nothing I can do about them now. I can wait as long as it takes. My sleep is good and so is my mood.

4. My friends and I have applied to (fill in the blank: *college/a job/a volunteer position*). We're supposed to hear back today.

    A. Everybody else seems cool with waiting, but I can barely make it through my first class. I'm feeling so overwhelmed. I'm checking my email and social media constantly. What if it's coming via snail mail? Maybe I should head home to intercept the mail.

    B. It's hard to concentrate on school, knowing that things will change if I get the response I want. Still, I take a deep breath and remind myself I'll know soon.

    C. As soon as I get to school, I'm so busy with my day, I hardly think about the application.

5. I'm in the middle of class, and I notice a strange lump on my arm.

   A. I immediately think the worst and text my parent to pick me up and take me to the doctor. I can't function. A zillion possibilities fly through my brain, and I can't stop searching for information online, so I know what I have and whether it can be treated immediately.

   B. Weird. That wasn't there yesterday, was it? I text my parent and ask them to schedule a medical appointment. I figure it's probably nothing and will wait to see the doctor.

   C. Weird. That wasn't there yesterday, was it? I must remember to ask my parent if I should see my doctor.

6. My friends want to hang out this weekend, and we start discussing plans at the end of the school day.

   A. Everybody seems fine deciding things at the last minute, and I hate that I'm not like that. I want us to make a firm and final plan now so I can relax. If I don't find out a few days in advance, I might not go at all.

   B. I'd prefer to make a firm and final plan now, but I get that my friends need to check in with others. It's annoying, but I'll go anyway.

   C. I'm fine with us taking our time. I can wait and play it by ear.

7. My family wants to try a new restaurant instead of going to our usual place.

   A. I immediately go online to view the menu and prepare. I have to know all my options and think carefully about the best thing to order.

   B. I start imagining the kinds of food they might serve and what type of entrée I might like. I hope it's as good as our usual place.

   C. I'm excited to try something new. I love surprises! I was getting bored by our usual place anyway.

8. We just finished our course selection planning, but it'll be another month before we know whether we get our first choice.

   A. A month is an eternity. I just don't think it's biologically possible for me to wait that long. I have to start planning my schedule for next year and prepare for each new teacher.

   B. A month is a long time to wait. I start imagining how it will go if I get my first choice, and if I don't.

   C. A month? A week? A day? It makes no difference because the new school schedule will be what it will be now or in a month from now.

9. I'm about to get a vaccine at school.

   A. I feel afraid of the pain and how I'll manage. Last time was awful, and that scene keeps replaying in my mind. What if I freak out in front of everyone?

   B. I don't like shots, and I'm pretty nervous about how this is gonna go, but I know I'll get through it.

   C. No one likes shots, but I can deal with it. This doesn't really bother me.

10. I heard my parents arguing late last night. They were loud, but I'm not sure what it was all about.

    A. I have to find out what this means. It could be a major crisis like they're gonna get a divorce! Perhaps we've run out of money? Is a family member ill? I'm too scared to ask them, but I will because I need to know so I can prepare.

    B. It sucks when people I care about fight, and it makes me sad. I wish I knew what it was about so I could help them.

    C. It sucks when people I care about fight, but it's not my business. If it concerns me, I'm sure I'll find out soon enough.

What's your score? Tally your responses as follows and add up your final score:

A = 3

B = 2

C = 1

Open to anything (Score = 10–12)

I'm pretty chill not knowing what's coming. Once in a while, I get snagged by a big thing, but otherwise, I'm cool with uncertainty.

Life is like a box of chocolates; you never know what you're gonna get.
—Forrest Gump

Middle of the road (Score = 13–22)

I like certainty about the big things, but generally don't sweat the little stuff. I know what's important and needs my time and attention, and what doesn't.

Sometimes, I get caught up in the drama of the little things and find I'm anxious, but generally, I can figure it out.

Be moderate in order to taste the joys of life in abundance.

—Epicurus

Love my GPS (Score = 23–30)

I need lots of certainty about everything: the big stuff and the little stuff. I get swept up in the unknowns, and this causes much stress and worry in my life. I wish it didn't happen this way, but it does.

Never quit certainty for hope.

—Scottish proverb

So now you know where things stand with how much certainty you crave. If you're an *open to anything* person, there is still a lot you can gain from this book. The strategies in each tip have been developed and tested on people with almost every single mental health condition, as well as medical conditions and many types of life problems, so odds are strongly in your favor that these strategies will help no matter what you're dealing with. If you're a *middle-of-the-road* type, but want to be less dependent on certainty, then these strategies will help you decrease your score and increase your tolerance of uncertainty. Finally, if you're a *love-my-GPS* teen, this book is exactly what you'll need to improve your strategies and help you be more confident to go with the flow of uncertainty!

TIP 1 TAKEAWAYS

In this tip, you learned the following:

- Certainty was fundamental to keeping our ancient ancestors alive, but modern life lacks the dangers we once faced. Unfortunately, fear of the negative unknowns has persisted and caused some of us to be intolerant of uncertainty, leading to daily distressing thoughts, feelings, and actions.

- Some of us crave more certainty than others because of our unique genetic, personality, and environmental experiences, or because we have an uncertainty allergy.

- The daily effects of struggling to cope with uncertainty are numerous, including seeing threats everywhere, having trouble problem solving and making decisions, and more.

- An adolescent's life is filled with ongoing unknowns and lacking in routine certainty. As a result, teens are more capable of managing uncertainty than at any other time in their lives simply because they have so much experience with it.

- The amount of certainty people need in their lives varies from person to person. The Tip 1 quiz shows how much certainty you need at the moment, but hopefully through the tips in this book, you will learn new ways to deal with life's unknowns so you can free yourself from overreliance on certainty.

This chapter's mission was to help you become an expert on understanding and being aware of uncertainty and how it affects you. How knowledgeable and aware are you about the effects of uncertainty now?

1	2	3	4	5
not much		*some*		*a lot*

Dropping the Uncertainty Struggle

This chapter's mission is to help you learn how to drop the struggle with uncertainty. How likely are you to allow unwanted thoughts and feelings of uncertainty to come and let them be?

1	*2*	*3*	*4*	*5*
not much		*some*		*a lot*

In addition to being a pioneer in discovering radiation and the first woman to win the Nobel Prize (and win it twice!), Marie Curie wisely said that life is full of struggles for all humans. Do you think that's true? We do! And in this tip, we will explain why dropping the struggle with uncomfortable thoughts, sensations, and emotions and learning to let them come and go just might be the path forward. This tip will help you

- understand that these unwanted thoughts and feelings are common experiences for all humans;

- learn that you can deal with them in more helpful ways;

- engage in fulfilling and meaningful activities while leaving such thoughts and feelings in the background.

WHY DO OUR BRAINS OVERTHINK?

As described in the previous tip, human beings are designed to be on the lookout for danger and seek comfort in certainty. Our brains are anticipation and problem-solving machines that constantly screen and search for things that may harm us, especially when situations are new or ambiguous (Grupe and Nitschke 2013). Whenever something uncertain shows up, even if it is small, our brains try to examine the event to make it more predictable, safer, and less uncomfortable for us. And then, to gain certainty, our brains analyze the situation some more. We call this overthinking and, while it can be annoying, the brain is just doing its job—which is thinking! This is very helpful when an uncertain situation represents danger or threat. For example, when walking in the woods, we want our brains to carefully analyze whether that mushroom is a chantarelle or a death cap. Or late at night before stepping onto the subway, it's important that we know for sure we're on the correct line. Sadly, for the rest of the time, when we're not facing danger or threat, there is no *off* button we can press when we no longer want to overthink.

And this happens with simple thinking too. If you've ever tried to meditate, you know what we mean. Within seconds of sitting still and being quiet, most of us experience our minds starting to wander and think about all sorts of random things. When we come to realize thinking is inevitable, it's easier to accept that we can't stop it. Your brain cannot help but finish these sentence openers: "Humpty Dumpty sat on the..." or "Roses are red, violets..." (Turrell and Bell 2016). And unfortunately, it's not just innocent nursery rhymes that cause our brains to generate words; when uncertainty strikes, our brains also start generating words and statements, such as "Everyone thinks I'm..." However, just because we don't have the power to stop our brains doesn't mean we have to sit there all day and listen to the constant overanalyzing or actively try to stop thinking those pesky thoughts. Instead, in this tip, you'll learn strategies to help you accept that this is what minds do and develop ways to move forward. But before we start, let's play a quick game to test out how difficult it is to make our brains suppress our thoughts or stop thinking about a specific thing.

DON'T THINK ABOUT THINKING

Get a piece of paper and a pencil or have your phone ready to record. We ask you to scratch your head gently, to stop, and then for one minute to focus as hard as you can and *don't* think about your head feeling itchy. Every time you think about it being itchy, tally it on your phone or paper. Remember, you are not supposed to think about scratching your head at all! Ready? Set? Go!

How many times did you think about scratching your head or feeling itchy? If this happened more than once, you now realize that just saying "don't think about it," ironically, makes your brain do the exact opposite. And this has been proven by research (Wegner et al. 1987). What happens is that our brains go on a mission to replace the "not-wanted" thought with another thought. And to do that, the brain must keep checking that the not-wanted thought is not there. So, while we may give our brain clear instructions not to think a specific thought, to suppress, and replace that thought, it literally has to keep thinking about it to make sure that you are following the "not think" instruction. Isn't this phenomenon ironic?

As you just learned, attempts to suppress a thought really don't work as a self-control strategy. So, what's the point in trying to fight thoughts you don't want to have if, in the end, you will think even more about these thoughts?

The same thing seems to happen with emotions. Has anyone ever told you not to be anxious or to stop worrying? Not very effective, right? As you have probably experienced, one of the tricks is to allow and keep feeling that emotion until enough time passes and the emotion disappears all on its own.

UNCERTAINTY ON A CONTINUUM

Now that you know that controlling thoughts (and feelings) is almost impossible, next you'll learn strategies to allow your thoughts and feelings to simply exist without having to fight with them. The first step is to recognize that overthinking or dealing with the unknown is a normal brain reaction to protect us (as described in Tip 1). The second step is to notice that the unwanted thoughts and feelings related to uncertainty can shift from being helpful (like when we face danger or important things) to unhelpful (the rest of the time).

UNHELPFUL  HELPFUL

Be aware that our difficulty tolerating uncertainty varies along a continuum. This means that instead of the fear being either absent or present, people dread the unknown in different degrees (Fergus and Carleton 2015). Remember when you first learned how to ride a bike or skateboard? Did you overthink what to do to prevent you from crashing? If you did, your mind was doing its job: it overfocused on the uncertain threats (for example, body position, balance, path, nearby people) and reacted in ways that reduced your chances of getting hurt, such as by tensing your body or making you very aware of your surroundings. These reactions were adaptive and beneficial because they likely helped you learn the new skill and protected you from danger. So, overthinking in this situation was more helpful than unhelpful on the uncertainty continuum. However, nothing is 100 percent certain, as you had probably fallen off several times despite being extremely careful. This is because sometimes our brains learn and remember better when we actually make mistakes. You'll read more about learning from mistakes in Tip 6.

Now, think about when bike riding or skateboarding became natural for you, and you no longer needed to be too careful. Earning a sense of freedom from all that hard learning probably felt good. However, this time, imagine that whenever you did something slightly more uncertain, like taking a different route or going over a bump, your brain overreacted and continued to send signals to your body, saying: "danger," "danger," "danger." But really, there wasn't any significant danger. Brains that overreact to potential threats unnecessarily and often are perceived as overly sensitive alert systems. And, as described in Tip 1, some anxious people may just have more hypervigilant brains that are less tolerant of uncertainty. Thus, this could just be part of their natural biological condition.

Because anxious brains are more likely to interpret uncertain situations as dangerous than nonanxious brains, they try to find ways to be safe that end up being unhelpful (Fergus and Carleton 2015). Wouldn't it be annoying if your brain kept trying to make you feel safe over and over again when you were trying to have fun biking or skateboarding? Like asking your parents to assure you you'd be safe, riding only on roads you had been to before, or not going out on your bike at all! Would you still want to explore cool places or practice new moves if your body freaked out every time you attempted something new? If you're like most of our clients, after a while, you'd stop exploring new places or trying new things because you'd get tired of hearing that danger signal all the time. And you might start to believe that biking or skateboarding was dangerous, as this sometimes was true in the past. Well, this is when uncertainty shifts and becomes unhelpful. In other words, the overly sensitive false alarm rings frequently and unnecessarily and gets in the way of letting you take upon new challenges, learn new skills, or do things that matter to you because it demands certainty before you can proceed.

AUTOMATIC ACTIONS: ARRS

Now that you know that you can't really stop a thought or feeling and that uncertainty varies along a continuum, our next strategy is to increase your awareness about the unhelpful and spontaneous actions we sometimes take when we feel threatened by uncertainty. When faced with uncertainty, people tend to feel stressed and anxious and, as a result, our brain's automatic response to reduce uncomfortable feelings and thoughts is to engage in specific actions that in psychology we call avoidance, reassurance seeking, rumination, or safety behaviors (aka ARRS).

Avoidance means purposely escaping or not engaging in situations that make you feel uncomfortable. These could include *not* talking to certain people, going to specific places, doing things that make you feel nervous or anxious such as public speaking or trying something new, and even procrastinating on an unpleasant task. In the research and clinical world, avoiding or getting rid of unwanted thoughts and feelings is called experiential avoidance and is considered a normal human psychological process (Hayes et al. 2006). In moderation, experiential avoidance is often harmless because there is some flexibility in our response to challenges and discomfort and, at times, it is even beneficial. But in excess, if we try to escape or get rid of uncomfortable thoughts and feelings a lot of the time, it may become a problem down the road because it will be harder for us to face new and important challenges that will make us grow and thrive in life.

To decrease the discomfort caused by uncertainty, we may also spontaneously engage in something called *reassurance seeking.* This may involve asking our parents, close friends, or teachers lots of questions to make sure that we are doing things right or having them repeatedly reassure us that we're not hurting anyone's feelings.

Another automatic AARS action to deal with uncertainty is *rumination.* When we ruminate, our brains replay scenes that happened in the past or imagine future scenarios to help us make sense of information and problem solve uncomfortable thoughts and feelings. Rumination is part of our brains' problem-solving function, but sometimes it doesn't really help us deal with uncertainty because we feel stuck rather than empowered to take action.

Finally, to avoid the discomfort caused by uncertainty, people may perform *safety behaviors*—doing extra things just to be sure that nothing bad will happen. Safety behaviors may include triple-checking your homework, overpreparing for presentations or conversations, only attending events with trusted or "safe" people, sitting at the back of the class or wearing neutral clothes to be less visible, or carrying items that reduce anxiety, such as a water bottle in case your throat feels tight.

AARS actions tend to reduce anxiety in the short run. However, these actions are not long-term solutions to dealing with the discomfort created by uncertain situations because the next time something uncertain comes up, you may need to spend even more time and energy performing one of the AARS actions in order to feel some relief. Thus, you may just get caught in a trap!

THE UNCERTAINTY TRAP

The uncertainty trap makes us deal with uncertain situations in unhelpful ways because getting rid of uncomfortable thoughts, feelings, and sensations by performing AARS actions provides some immediate relief. However, this relief doesn't last very long and, in fact, can make things worse in the long run. Let's see how this works using the example of Pedro, who believed that avoidance and playing it safe worked well, but then realized that trying to gain certainty moved him away from his life goals.

Meet Pedro

I'm Pedro (he/him), and I'm in eighth grade in a small rural middle school. I've got many friends at school and love playing soccer, reading sci-fi books, listening to pop music, and drawing. Even though I like spending time with my friends at school and feel that they trust me, I have a hard time sharing personal things about myself with them. Like, my buddies have no idea that I like books and spend hours every weekend reading rather than playing video games. They also have no clue that I'm good at drawing and take part in an online drawing club for teens. What I'm most embarrassed to share with them is my taste for music. I feel like if they knew that I like K-pop, they would think I'm a wimp. They might make fun of me and even not want to hang out with me anymore.

Because I worry about what others think about me, I don't talk much about myself with them, and I change subjects when they ask me personal questions. When my friends come to hang out at my house, I hide my drawing supplies and remove my drawings hanging on the wall. If they ask me about music, I just pretend that I don't listen to music at all.

I find that not opening up and showing who I am for real makes my worries about being judged go away for a while, and I feel better in the moment. At the same time though, I also feel disconnected from my friends and kind of alone because they don't know who I really am. I notice that the more I hide my true self, the more I worry about being myself in front of others. For example, I used to enjoy listening to music and talking about the books I read with my family, but now, I no longer feel comfortable doing that. Also, I used to post my drawings on an online drawing platform. Now I worry that people will know who I am, so I no longer post anything online.

If I look back at how this all started, it seems that it used to be a little, insignificant worry that didn't really get in the way. But now it feels like it is taking over my life because I'm always watching what I say. Socializing exhausts me, and I end up spending most of my free time alone in my room.

Below is a diagram of the uncertainty trap using Pedro's story. It shows that a specific situation leads to uncomfortable thoughts and feelings that result in automatic ARRS actions followed by relief.

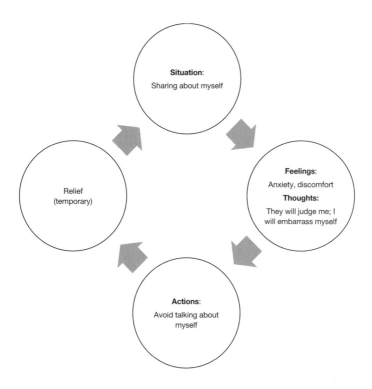

As you can see, when a situation with an unpredictable outcome comes up, like Pedro having the opportunity to share about his favorite song or love for drawing, uncertain thoughts about how his friends will react and unpleasant feelings show up. To deal with the discomfort of not knowing the outcome, Pedro decided to avoid saying anything or to engage in safety behaviors such as only giving minimal or neutral information about himself. Avoiding or playing it safe worked for Pedro in the short run because he felt relieved in the moment and didn't have to deal with his fear of judgment or embarrassment for a while. But by putting things off to protect himself from the bad stuff, Pedro also stopped himself from enjoying the good stuff, like having fun with his friends and feeling connected.

It's important to remember that if, like Pedro, we try to escape or get rid of uncomfortable thoughts and feelings a lot of the time, it may become a problem down the road because it will be harder for us to face new and important challenges that will make us grow and thrive in life.

Bottom line: *although struggling with thoughts and feelings when facing the unknown is a normal thing that all brains do, there are better ways to deal with it.*

Next, we'll show you how using the waves of uncertainty analogy and practicing the SOS skills can help you better deal with uncertainty than engaging in ARRS actions.

WAVES OF UNCERTAINTY

Imagine that you're going for a swim in the ocean on a hot day. The waves seem small from where you are, and you're excited to get closer and try to catch one. As you approach them, you realize that they're bigger and stronger than you first anticipated. Even though you're a good swimmer, a giant wave picks up and breaks right on top of you, sweeping you under the water. How would you react in this situation? If you're like most people, you would panic and try to get up for air. The problem is the waves keep coming, and the more you struggle with each wave, the more oxygen and energy you use up, and the more likely you are to continue to be tossed around like a rag doll. Believe it or not, the most helpful thing to do in situations like that goes against our "caveperson" instincts. Rather than fighting the wave, you should tell yourself to relax, or like surfers say, "hold down," under the water, and wait until the wave passes. Weird, isn't it? But it actually works!

When dealing with uncertain situations, we can use the same technique surfers do. Rather than fighting with the uncertainty waves filled with uncomfortable thoughts, feelings, and sensations, we can acknowledge that they are there and will pass in their own time. Just like waves in the ocean, thoughts, feelings, and sensations come and go, even though sometimes they seem bigger and last longer than we expect.

SOS SKILLS

In the next paragraphs, you'll learn about three great skills to help you drop the struggle with uncertainty. The first one (slowing down) will teach you how to calm your body when its sensitive alarm system goes off. The second strategy (observing) will help you disengage from uncomfortable thoughts and feelings, and then observe and let them pass by in their own time. The final technique (shifting) will teach you to ground yourself when faced with the unknown and to take meaningful actions. We hope you enjoy and practice the SOS techniques whenever you need them, instead of engaging in ARRS actions.

Skill #1: Slowing Down

Has anyone ever taught you deep breathing? Did it work for you? Even if you didn't find it helpful, please hear us out. We personally also used to have a hard time with this strategy because it requires time, patience, concentration, and especially practice. However, as we learned more about how helpful this skill can be to calm down our bodies and minds, and practiced different types of breathing, we found the ones that worked for us. We're sure you already know how to breathe; otherwise, you wouldn't be alive! So, we don't need to teach you how to take slow and deep breaths through your nose and exhale the air through your mouth. Even if you believe that deep breathing isn't for you, you might find it interesting to know why it's such a popular technique.

Remember how our bodies react when our brains perceive a threat? We tend to breathe shallowly and quickly from our chest, and our muscles tense up as if we were doing some hard-core exercise. The trick is to help our bodies gradually calm down by breathing slowly so we can better think and deal with anxiety-provoking situations in more effective ways. There are tons of different deep breathing exercises. Based on our experience, we have selected a few that our teen clients like the best, and we hope you will too. We suggest you try them all and then decide which one you are most likely to do. Just before we start, please remember: deep breathing tends to work best if you practice it *frequently* and while you are *not feeling anxious*. It might also be easier to combine breathing with daily activities you're already doing such as taking a shower, going for a walk, or lying in bed. That way, it will feel less like a chore and be easier to remember to do. If, after this section, you still think that deep breathing is not for you, that's okay! We'll share other skills to help you drop the struggle with uncertainty in this tip.

Take-Me-to-That-Place Breathing

We invite you to look through the photo gallery on your phone, a photo album at home, or even on the internet to find a picture of your favorite place in nature. It doesn't have to be a place you've been to, but it helps if you have. Take a few moments to select the image.

Now while you look at this picture, take deep breaths for two to three minutes or so. There is no need to try to breathe in a specific way or teach yourself how to breathe. Just breathe naturally and let your mind take you to that spot. Focus on the image, noticing all the details about it as you breathe in and as you breathe out. Without resisting any thoughts, notice how your body and your mind feel as you look at this picture and breathe. How did you feel?

Breathing Music

For this activity, select a song that you really enjoy. After you find the song, get into a comfortable position, put your headphones on, and listen to it while breathing naturally. Listen to the whole song before you stop this exercise. Focus on sounds the instruments make or the tone and rhythm of the vocals, noticing all the variation you can hear as you breathe in and as you breathe out. What did you notice?

Hand Breathing

In this breathing exercise, you'll use your hand as you breathe in and out. Using one pointer finger, trace the outline of your other hand, finger by finger, as you breathe in, pause, and breathe out. Take a moment to observe how you feel as you practice this exercise tracing both hands.

Daydream Breathing

This next exercise has no script. In your room, close your eyes and let yourself daydream while breathing naturally for two to three minutes or so. Focus on all the images your mind creates as you breathe in and as you breathe out. What did you think about? How did you feel?

Skill #2: Observing

Another skill to help drop the struggle between you and uncertainty is to visualize thoughts or sensations coming and going at their own pace. In other words, you observe them as occurring outside of you so that you can see them rather than feel them. The *passing on by* strategy works by noticing thoughts, images, or sensations and placing them on things or objects that move at their own pace, like leaves, clouds, or musical notes. The more you practice noticing (versus feeling) your thoughts and sensations related to uncertainty and letting them pass by in their own time, the less likely you are to struggle with them.

For example, imagine that you and some other people were invited to hang out at your friend's house this weekend. You're excited to go, but you don't know who is coming for sure. There's a possibility that your close friend has basketball practice and won't come, and that some people you don't really know will be there. First, you start having thoughts such as, *What if I don't know anyone there? What if nobody talks to me?* Then, your brain begins to problem solve whether the hangout is safe to go to. At the same time, you start feeling your chest tighten and your heart beating faster. What would you do in a situation like that? You could use the *passing on by* strategy and notice those thoughts as clouds in the sky or ants on the ground. Here are two examples we use with clients, but you can also use your imagination to create your own.

Swipe the Thought

Think about a situation that made you feel somewhat uncomfortable or uncertain this week. Think about a few words that represent your unwanted thoughts, sensations, and feelings. Now imagine that you are looking through a photo album on your phone. In your mind, place the thoughts or feelings in separate photo frames and swipe them, one by one. Continue doing this exercise as thoughts come to your mind. Let them be there for a bit and then swipe. What did you notice?

Clouds in the Sky

Another idea is to drop the struggle by placing thoughts and sensations of uncertainty in clouds passing by in the sky. As we know, even during a rainy season, clouds (and rain) come and go in their own time even when it feels like they will take forever to move past. In your mind, think of some unwanted thoughts and sensations, and imagine them passing on by in their own time. What did you notice?

Skill #3: Shifting

This is the last skill to help you drop the struggle between you and uncertainty. Shifting is exactly what it sounds like: you shift away from focusing on uncertainty, worry, or stress, and put your time and attention on the things that matter. Please note that this is *not* a distraction technique, but rather an exercise that makes you aware of what's going on inside and outside you and directs you to take some helpful action. In brief, each letter of CALM refers to a specific action you will take to center yourself when something challenging or overwhelming shows up, and you don't want to act on impulse or avoid it. The goal is to work through each letter in order from C to M, like this:

C = Check in with what's going on inside you: Take a deep breath and notice what is going on inside you. What is your mind saying to you, and what sensations are you feeling? Where in your body do you feel the sensations?

A= Activate your body: do a little stretch, move your shoulders backward, squeeze your fists, or press one hand against the other in a way to feel your body and gain a sense of control and confidence that you're in charge.

L= Look and listen to what's happening outside you: Be curious and open about your surroundings. Notice five things you see, three sounds you hear, and two things you can touch.

M= Make your actions meaningful: Get up and go do something meaningful, or something that makes you feel good or meets your needs. For example, call a friend, go for a run, drink warm tea, listen to music, or take a bubble bath.

Repeat the steps above a few times in a row to help you memorize the sequence. Remember, the more you practice, the easier it will become. This coming week, we invite you to use CALM during one event related to an uncertain situation that makes you feel uncomfortable, and write down what you noticed, either on your phone or in a journal.

TIPS FOR PRACTICE

We encourage you to schedule at least five minutes per day to practice the SOS skills described in this tip. To help you remember to practice, please put reminders on your phone or planner and record your performance for the next week in the notes app on your phone or a journal. Below is an example of how to track your SOS practice:

Date	Strategy	Duration	Outcome
7/30	Swipe the thought	5 minutes	Felt more relaxed
7/31	CALM	2 minutes	Got homework done!
8/1	Breathing music	10 minutes	Did my presentation online

It's time to wrap up! Life is not easy, and we all have a natural tendency to fight against unwanted thoughts and feelings in hopes of getting rid of them and feeling better. In this tip, you learned about the reasons behind our struggles with uncertainty and how they can be helpful versus unhelpful and, at times, get in the way of a teen's life (by engaging in ARRS actions). The good news is that, despite such struggles being part of humanity, the SOS skills can help you cope with the unknown by allowing uncertainty to come and be, while you do things that matter to you. In the next tip, we will share some strategies to help you improve your relationship with uncertainty.

TIP 2 TAKEAWAYS

In Tip 2, you learned the following:

- Life is full of struggles for all human beings. There is no point in fighting thoughts (and feelings) because the more you don't want them, the more you will have them. Instead, just let them be!

- Our difficulty tolerating uncertainty varies along a continuum from helpful to unhelpful depending on the situation.

- When we try to protect ourselves from potential bad outcomes, like avoiding or doing things in excess (ARRS actions), we end up missing out on the good stuff and falling into a trap.

- Just like waves in the ocean, thoughts and feelings come and go, even though sometimes they seem bigger and last longer than we expect.

- The goal is to drop the struggle with unwanted thoughts and feelings by practicing the SOS skills. These include breathing, letting thoughts come and go, and grounding ourselves to take meaningful actions toward things that are important or matter to you.

This chapter's mission was to help you learn how to drop the struggle with uncertainty. How likely are you now to allow unwanted thoughts and feelings of uncertainty to come and let them be?

1	2	3	4	5
not much		*some*		*a lot*

Making Friends with Uncertainty: Becoming Frenemies!

This chapter's mission is to build a case to support that uncertainty doesn't have to be our enemy and might even be a friend. How likely are you to consider uncertainty a friend?

1	2	3	4	5
not much		*some*		*a lot*

Fun fact! A 2019 study at Pennsylvania State University found that 91 percent of the things people worry about don't come true. And when the feared things did happen, about a third of participants found the outcome was better than expected (LaFreniere and Newman 2019). So how can this information help us?

To begin with, it tells us that if you're worrying about things like missing out on a social event, getting a bad mark on an assignment, or something bad happening to your family, these things are very unlikely to happen. We mean 91 percent unlikely! And yet, if you're reading this book, you probably worry quite a bit about unknown *negative* future events, and you're not alone. In fact, people who struggle with a lot of anxiety have two things in common: (1) they worry that bad things are likely to happen to them, and (2) they believe that when those bad things happen, they won't be able to cope. But the Penn State study tells us that if you're worrying about a bad thing happening to you, maybe you don't have to worry quite as much because, *most* of the time, the bad thing never even happens. And even if it does happen, chances are it won't be exactly as you expected.

At the start of this tip, we asked how likely you are to consider uncertainty your friend, and our guess is that you probably chose a low rating. But why is that? Given research that has shown that 91 percent of the things most of us worry about don't come true, why do some of us consider uncertainty as the enemy? For many people, it's because coping with uncertainty doesn't feel good. And some of us blow out of proportion the possibility that the remaining 9 percent chance of something bad happening will actually come to pass. But does uncertainty really result in negative outcomes for you *personally?* Let's find out.

FRIEND OR FOE?

Using a journal or the notes section in your phone, look at the examples below and create a few of your own by tracking both some recent worries you've just had (past events) and some worries about things that will come up in the next week or two (future events). Then check off whether these worries come true. Make sure you choose events that are specific, measurable, and observable so that you can tell whether they actually happen.

Worries from the past:

> What I worried about: *My friends at my old school would be so busy having fun that they wouldn't text me during the school week now that I'm at a new school.*

What happened: *They didn't text for a few days, but then I got a bunch of messages from them asking how I was doing and letting me know they missed me.*

Did my worry come true? _____ Yes __X__ No

Worries about future events:

What I worried about: *I'll get into a fight with my dad about my negative attitude toward my new school.*

What happened: *He told me to stop talking down about my new school, but we didn't fight.*

Did my worry come true? _____Yes __X__ No

Add up the number of events that never happened and divide your answer by the total number of events. Multiply by 100. This is your percentage score. For example: 9 (events that never happened) ÷10 (total number of events) x100 = 90 percent, leaving you with a 10 percent chance of a bad event happening.

Is your score as high as 91 percent? And if not quite that high, is it higher than 75 percent or even 60 percent? If your score is anywhere close to the Penn State study, we have our first piece of evidence to support that uncertainty doesn't need to be our enemy because the unknown future events often turn out just fine and aren't negative after all. Uncertainty really isn't the bad guy. But if we're going to change your mind, we think we'll need more evidence to build a strong case. So, let's get going!

THE WIZARD OF OZ EFFECT

If you've read or seen *The Wizard of Oz*, you may remember that, throughout the story, Dorothy and her friends are searching for the Wizard of Oz because they believe he is powerful and all-knowing and has the answers they seek. However, when they eventually reach the Emerald City, they discover that the wizard is simply a regular guy doing a job, with no special power. This story reminds us that it's easy to build up things in our minds as being bigger or more important than they really are.

Have you ever inflated the importance of an event or pumped it up in size, only to realize later on it wasn't such a big deal as the event shrunk to a more manageable level? In fact, our brains can spend hours imagining how a situation will unfold when the situation itself is only minutes long. For example, how long would you worry about approaching a crush to ask them on a date or confronting a friend with an important concern? Even though these interactions will only last minutes, we can spend hours or even days worrying about them.

This is one example of how the power of uncertainty can seem grand: it convinces us that the unknown possibilities are dreadful and we won't be able to cope, when the reality is far less sinister. So, if we can shift our thinking and recognize uncertainty isn't this huge deal, just like the Wizard of Oz turned out to be a regular guy, uncertainty no longer needs to be our enemy but just a routine part of our lives. The question is: has uncertainty got you magnifying little hassles into earth-shattering events and causing you to view it as the enemy?

FROM MAGNIFY TO MINIMIZE: SHRINKING WORRIES

Try this: Reflect about some worries you've had during the past year. Identify one worry for each of these time points: today, last week, last month, last term, and last year. To describe the size of your worry, you can use this range: *cookie crumb, Lego, sandwich, backpack, car, house, airplane, mountain.* Then, using your journal or phone, write down your responses to the following questions. We've included sample responses in italics to help you get started.

What was your worry? *I was afraid I would fail my math final.*

When did you have this worry? *Last term*

What was your experience then? *The more I focused on it, the bigger my worry became. By the end of the term, the worry was as big as a house.*

Were you magnifying or minimizing your worry? *Magnifying*

What do you think now? *As I think back on it now, it was actually as big as a backpack.*

What did you notice? Perhaps a few of your worries were bigger to start with. But, after the situation passed and you reflected on it, you realized it wasn't nearly as big and terrible as you first thought. Maybe this happened with all your examples.

When it comes to managing uncertainty, we may blow things out of proportion and build them up to be the size of a mountain. Magnifying this way can leave us feeling small, powerless, and unable to cope. However, like the Wizard of Oz, anxiety and uncertainty don't have to hold a special power over us and be the enemy we once presumed. Instead, anxiety and uncertainty have an important job: to warn and protect us from danger and prepare us for important events. That's it! No more, no less. Therefore, if we can learn to coexist with anxiety and uncertainty (versus pushing them away), something that once seemed powerful suddenly shrinks to a more manageable size. Perhaps this concept can give us the second piece of evidence: *if we keep uncertainty in perspective, it doesn't have to be a powerful enemy.*

Next, we will continue to build our case for why uncertainty isn't our enemy and might even be our friend.

YOU'RE STRONGER THAN YOU THINK!

When I (Katherine) was learning to swim, I was too scared to go in farther than up to my waist because I thought I would sink. Even though my parents tried to convince me I was fine, and signed me up for swim lessons, I just wouldn't budge. Up to my waist was all I would do! Then one day, my grandma came to stay, and we went swimming. She explained that our lungs naturally hold air so that when we lie back in the water, we always float. Turns out, it's not biologically possible to sink as we have a natural floating device built right into our bodies. When I learned this, I was then free to swim without fear because I had what it took within me the whole time. I still swim three times a week to this day and love it!

Many of us can recall times when we initially thought we couldn't do something, like riding a bike, skating a half-pipe, or baking a soufflé, but then we did it. And the reason why is that we had it in us all along, but simply didn't realize it. Has there been an activity or situation where you didn't believe in yourself only to discover that you had it in you all along?

If you remembered a personal example, you may be wondering what my story and your story have to do with the possibility of befriending uncertainty. Well, as you will discover below, you already possess some natural abilities in your brain to calm the anxiety that often accompanies uncertainty. So, rather than being afraid of uncertainty and viewing it as the enemy, we'd like to encourage you to allow uncertainty to give you the opportunity to use the skills you already possess.

As you read in the prior section, although our brains can magnify small events and get us worked up and highly anxious, our brains can also calm us down. As you will see in the two strategies that follow, we possess some great abilities to cope through anxious moments, and this highlights that it's possible to view uncertain situations or events as opportunities for growth and learning, permitting uncertainty to be our friend!

Skill #1: The Translation Switch

The translation switch is a useful strategy to help calm the mind when uncertainty stirs up trouble. This strategy highlights how coping with difficult experiences, like uncertainty, begins in the brain, and focuses on how the brain shares and integrates information. As you may know, the brain is divided into two hemispheres, the right and the left, which communicate with one another to ensure the smooth functioning of our daily lives. The right brain is the *feeling* side that gathers information through our senses and deals with emotions and nonverbal information (for example, facial expressions, gestures, tone, body posture). The left brain is the *logical and analytical* side that deals with facts, logic, and language. Both sides work as a team to communicate the information either receives to the other and then to translate and integrate it to help us make decisions that ensure we live balanced, holistic, and valued lives. If we only felt things (right side), we would be a seething mass of emotions and senses making it nearly impossible to get things done. And if we only worked with logic (left side), we would be a rigid fact machine unable to flex to meet the variable demands of our lives. Fortunately, our brain is sophisticated enough that both sides can share and integrate information to help us in many ways, including coping with difficult experiences like managing uncertainty. Read about Brianna's first day at her new high school and see if you can spot her right and left hemispheres in action.

Meet Brianna

Hey, I'm Brianna (she/her). My family and I recently moved from one part of the city to another. Although I can keep in touch with my close friends on weekends, starting at a brand-new high school has been hard because I don't know anyone. On my first day, I realized I'd been given the wrong schedule and was late getting to my first class. Then, halfway through that class, another kid got sick and almost vomited. Seeing someone throw up always makes me feel like it might happen to me, and I was so worried that I could barely concentrate on what the teacher was saying. I spent the rest of the day worrying that I might vomit.

At lunch, I realized I didn't have enough money to buy lunch and only ate an apple and some chips from the vending machine. By the time I got home that afternoon, I was exhausted, hungry, scared, frustrated, and sad at having to be at this new school. My brain was firing worry messages at me one after another like a bad volleyball game: What if tomorrow is worse than today? What if I never make friends? Will I get sick like that kid? It's not fair! I'll never catch up in science after spacing out this morning. *I went straight to my room, climbed into bed, and burst into tears. I decided I'd skip school tomorrow.*

Later on, when my mom got back from work, we talked about my day. My mom helped me see that my right brain was filled with negative thoughts, and scary predictions, and feelings like anxiety and fear, which had led me to give up and hide in my bed. She helped me get to my left brain with some useful facts: that the first day of a new school is always hard, that I've now got the right class schedule and lunch money so tomorrow, I'll be prepared. As soon as I listened to my left brain, my right brain calmed down and I realized that I could go back to school.

The straightforward act of talking something through is a central part of many forms of psychotherapy and cultural healing practices and is one of the ways humans can recover from trauma and difficult life experiences. When we talk or tell about what has happened, this act allows the feelings side of our brain to communicate with the logical side and then translate this information into a coping/action plan. This process is at the heart of the translation switch strategy.

For example, as Brianna labeled her feelings, talked about her many experiences, and recalled the tsunami of anxious thoughts, her left brain was doing its job: translating this information into logic and facts to organize and make sense of her experiences. It reminded her how she had coped through these difficulties and what she could do to prepare to try again. Her left and right sides worked together to help calm her thoughts and feelings.

The next time you notice being struck by worry and uncertainty, start by observing and naming your emotions. Are you scared? Worried? Anxious? Mad? If you don't know the exact feeling, you can also describe your body sensations, like a knot in the stomach or pressure in the chest. Then try talking about it with a trusted person to integrate the right and left sides and translate this information into an action plan. Who might you choose? Take a few minutes and think about three people who can serve as your trusted helpers.

Skill #2: Mini Translation Switch

Sometimes uncertainty can ambush us with little warning. A teacher calls a pop quiz, your friend accuses you of lying, or your parent texts you to come home immediately. Suddenly, your feelings side of the brain floods you with a rapid onset of emotions, unpleasant bodily sensations, and urges to escape or avoid. For some, this could occur in the form of a panic attack. When this happens, you may not find time to integrate the feelings and logic parts of your brain by chatting with a friend or talking it through by yourself. Instead, these situations require immediate action. The mini version of the translation switch provides a way to rapidly make sense of what's happening, translates this information into a plan, and helps calm you as you ride out the uncertain/anxious/panic wave to shore.

In these situations, you will identify your emotion and then create a label, or any short phrase, that explains what's happening. It can be anything that makes sense to you, and in fact, the fewer the words and simpler the label, the easier it will be to remember when you really need it. For example:

- (I'm afraid.) *That's my panic tsunami trying to knock me over.*

- (I'm worried.) *There goes my DJ brain, spinning worry tunes 24/7.*

- (I'm feeling edgy.) *I'm a snappin' turtle. Stay clear, everyone!*

Although the unexpected means we have no advance notice and cannot prepare, some teens become aware of a theme to how they feel, think, and act whenever uncertainty strikes, and even though the situations change, the theme stays the same; for example, always assuming the worst, or being really mean and judgmental to themselves. Others tend to run away or escape at the first sight of difficulty or to doubt their own abilities to cope. If a theme shows up, you can pick a label ahead of time and have it ready to go. These are some common examples some of our clients have chosen:

- When worry strikes, it's *Worst-case-Wendy on the scene.*

- Here goes my overreactor again!

- I'm like a deer caught in the headlights!

- When I'm mad, I join the *it's not fair, why me, you suck* gang.

Now it's your turn. You can personalize your situation better than we can! Have you noticed any themes to how you respond when uncertainty strikes? If so, try to come up with one or two labels that capture the integration and translation experience of your feelings side with the logical side of your brain to help calm you in uncertainty emergencies. Use your journal or phone to write these down so you won't forget.

Hopefully, you now have a name or phrase for when uncertainty strikes and stirs up an emotional tsunami. Your job is to start noticing when these situations arise and to label or identify how you feel or how they impact you. As soon as you do this, you might think through what's happened or talk with someone about it to help translate your experience(s). Or simply label it. In thinking about, talking through, or labeling your uncertainty, you're activating your logical brain and asking it to communicate with your feelings side of the brain. With the integration of both sides, your systems can start to translate what has happened and help calm you with an action plan.

If you think this strategy may help, then this becomes our third and final piece of evidence in favor of becoming friends with uncertainty. Befriending uncertainty in this way means our relationship can shift from one of seeing uncertainty as the enemy to seeing it as an opportunity to use our own strengths (our right and left brains) to get through difficult situations and thrive. Uncertainty becomes a gift from a friend!

FRIEND, ENEMY, OR FRENEMY?

With the knowledge and awareness you now have about worry and uncertainty, we wonder if you might be willing to reconsider your relationship with them. Maybe you have some evidence that uncertainty isn't your enemy after all, and even if you're not quite ready to be friends with it, you can call a truce and be frenemies. So perhaps it's time for a new perspective: try viewing uncertainty as something that exists, but doesn't need to control us or direct how we feel, kind of like a nosy neighbor or annoying car alarm. These things exist in our communities, but we don't have to pay them much attention. When your nosy neighbor waves you over to talk on your walk home from school, you know if you start chatting, they'll be following you home every day. Instead, you'd offer a polite hello and keep walking. So how about treating uncertainty the same way. Notice it, but carry on with all the other more important things in your day. When uncertainty strikes, there's no point in letting it direct our emotional compass for the day.

TIP 3 TAKEAWAYS

In this tip, you learned the following:

- Perhaps being afraid of uncertainty isn't so helpful, as most of the time, the unknowns aren't actually bad or harmful. And most of the things we worry about never even come true!

- Like the Wizard of Oz, anxiety and uncertainty don't have to hold a special power over us. We tend to magnify the importance and meaning of uncertainty when, in reality, it's usually small and manageable and something we are equipped to manage.

- Coping with uncertainty requires both sides of our brain to communicate by combining the information we get from our feelings (the right side) with logic and facts (the left side). To do this, we need to either talk through the uncertainty we face with others or ourselves or use a label (like naming the emotion you're feeling in the moment). The translation switch strategy helps make sense of unexpected stressful events and leads to a calmer body and mind.

This chapter's mission was to build a case to support that uncertainty doesn't have to be our enemy and might even be a friend. How likely are you to consider uncertainty a friend now?

1	2	3	4	5
not much		some		a lot

TIP 4

Creating Space Between You and Uncertainty

This chapter's mission is to help you make space between you and the uncertainty you encounter in daily life by learning to coexist with uncertainty without it causing unnecessary stress, worry, and suffering. How able are you to create space in your life for uncertainty?

1	*2*	*3*	*4*	*5*
not much		*some*		*a lot*

How many times has someone told you "Life's not fair!" or have you found yourself doing something you didn't really enjoy? Most of us do things that we would prefer not to do every day (like getting up early to go to school or taking the garbage out) in service of something bigger like graduating from school or helping others out. Have you recently done any of the following?

- Dragged yourself out of a warm bed to get to school

- Taken a test

- Cleaned up your room

- Scooped the dog poo/cleaned up after a pet

- Washed a sink full of dishes or loaded the dishwasher

- Gone to the dentist or doctor

- Received a vaccination

- Went for a run or walk in cold or wet weather

If you have done even just a few of these things, you're familiar with doing things you didn't like or want to do, but were willing to do because you knew it was necessary or perhaps good for you in the long run. There's a difference between willing and wanting (Harris 2019). And when it comes to uncertainty, it's clear you might not want the experience, but we hope you'll soon discover that you might be more willing to accept it than you initially thought.

Dealing with uncertainty is a lot like having a flu shot or taking a test: we can allow it to be part of our lives even though it's not what we like or want because it is in the service of something greater and more meaningful to us. So, when we accept uncertainty, we must do so completely; there's no halfway version, just like there's no partial flu shot or half test. Bottom line: uncertainty is an on-and-off phenomenon; we either accept it or we don't (Turrell and Bell 2016). In this tip, you will discover that by being willing to make space for uncertainty, even though you might not want it, life actually becomes easier and more enjoyable.

UNCERTAINTY IS EVERYWHERE

As you learned in Tip 1, uncertainty exists in many areas of teen life, and it's inescapable. We face uncertainty from the moment we wake up to the depths of our sleep, and its outcome can range from insignificant to life-changing. *Will there be enough milk for my cereal? Will I miss the bus? Have my friends forgotten about the post I made yesterday? Will I pass the test? Is my mom's cancer treatable? Will my dad get a job? Will I have that nightmare again?*

Your answer to all of these is probably *I don't know.* And no one knows because the future hasn't happened yet and until it does, it remains unknown. For some of us, this is where stress, worry, and anxiety come in. The less we know, the more we may suffer when we struggle against the inherent uncertainty in our lives. But as we learned in Tip 2, struggling with uncertainty by trying to avoid or control it doesn't really work for most people, so perhaps it's time to consider dropping the struggle and trying something new. Let's learn about Arjun, who tried to control his life to make things predictable for years and then realized that coexisting with uncertainty was the way to go to have a lighter and more enjoyable time.

Meet Arjun

I'm Arjun (he/him). I've struggled with stress and anxiety since middle school, and when I got into my final year of high school, I was feeling burned out. I knew it was a bad sign to be exhausted before college even began. For years, I'd tried to plan out everything down to the last detail to help me succeed. This meant: keeping one step ahead of my friends with trends, fashion, and music so I was always in control; spending hours on school assignments to avoid low marks and disappointing my teachers and family; and keeping my feelings in check to never let on how scared I often felt. I sometimes thought it was what it must be like to be a boxer: always having to dodge the unexpected and stay on top, except, unlike a boxing match that lasts less than an hour, this was my constant.

But one day, things changed when I ran across a podcast interview with a mindfulness expert who spoke about the art of being open and acting with purpose. In listening, I discovered that if I opened up and made space to accept that uncertainty would always exist no matter what I did, and instead put my energy into doing things that mattered, life would be inherently less stressful. I realized I'd spent years trying to control or avoid, but only felt trapped and confined, which was in direct contrast to how open and free I felt when I accepted and made space for uncertainty.

After I got accepted by the college I had always dreamed about, I continued to dislike when things were uncertain, but now I respond differently. I can catch myself struggling with it and practice creating space between myself and these stressors and then I put my energy toward doing things that actually matter.

We'd like to offer you the alternative of making space like Arjun did, rather than trying to control or avoid things and continuing to struggle with uncertainty (or getting caught in the uncertainty trap as discussed in Tip 2). The first step is to accept that uncertainty is everywhere, the future is unknown, *and* this is not a bad or dangerous thing. In fact, unknowns are things anyone can learn to handle if we are open to and *willing* for uncertainty to exist in our lives even if we don't always *want* it.

Skill #1: Making Space

Dr. Russ Harris, an Australian medical practitioner and psychotherapist, has created hundreds of techniques he shares in videos, books, and trainings, including an exercise called expansion (Harris 2008, 2019). This exercise is designed to help us make room for the difficult internal experiences like feelings, sensations, memories, thoughts, and urges that accompany uncertainty. Rather than continuing to waste our energy trying to fight with uncertainty, the aim is to expand, or make space, for it. Dr. Harris is a practitioner of acceptance and commitment therapy (ACT), a well-researched therapy that helps people identify what matters to them, leading them to change unhelpful behaviors in order to live their lives with purpose, even as they experience uncomfortable thoughts, feelings, and sensations. Through the research of Dr. Harris and other practitioners of ACT, we have increasing evidence to support that when we stop struggling with difficult internal experiences and instead simply make space for them, something interesting and unexpected happens: the difficult experiences disrupt our lives less, not more (Harris 2008).

To see how this works, try the following four-step activity and see what happens.

Start by finding a quiet spot where you won't be interrupted, and get comfortable. Turn off your phone, put a "Shhh" sign on your door, or tell the people in your house you need five minutes of privacy.

Step 1: Observe

As you are starting to get comfortable, try to notice how your body feels. Ideally, it's best to do this exercise when you're dealing with uncertainty in real time.

- Isolate a single area or sensation in your body and hyperfocus on it.

- Use the noticing part of your mind to observe how the uncertainty feels in that part of your body: Does it feel tight? Heavy? Painful? Achy? Tingly? Something else?

- Imagine this area or sensation as an object, floating in front of you in three-dimensional space. What color is it? Size? Shape? Texture? Weight? Smell? Sound? Does it move?

Step 2: Breathe

Close your eyes and take a few breaths in and out, noticing how the air travels as you breathe. Focus on your uncertainty sensation and send your breath to that location. You are not trying to breathe away these sensations but to use the breath to steady yourself. If your mind wanders, simply acknowledge its distractibility and return to breathing in and out.

Step 3: Expand

Continue to breathe, and as you do so, imagine your breath expanding within you, traveling around your uncertainty sensation or object, surrounding it fully and completely. Your breath expands to coat this sensation or object, creating an invisible membrane or bubble between you and it, acting as a buffer. If your mind wanders, simply bring your attention back to this exercise.

Step 4: Allow

As you continue to breathe, notice that you can feel more comfortable and confident that your uncertainty can coexist within you without affecting you. It's like having something in your pocket that you're aware of, but it doesn't change what you do or how you feel. By permitting uncertainty to have space in your body, you notice that it no longer has as much power over you and cannot boss you about. Take a few more breaths and then gradually return your gaze to the outside space and open your eyes. Thank your mind for taking you on this journey.

Now that you know how to *make space,* the objective is to use these four steps whenever uncertainty pops up and creates difficult feelings or sensations. In those moments, use your breath to expand the space between you and your uncertainty, creating a protective membrane that buffers you from getting pulled into the vortex of stress, worry, and fear. When you do this, you increase your ability to coexist with these difficult feelings or sensations without them having control over you. And having space, rather than feeling trapped, can help you make wise and purposeful decisions about how you want to proceed rather than impulsive ones you end up regretting. So, let's learn more about how to do that.

UNCERTAINTY IS A BODGIT... BUT WAIT, WHAT'S A BODGIT?

Imagine you're going somewhere fun. It could be a short outing for the afternoon, a weekend trip to your grandma's, or a longer vacation somewhere you've been wanting to go. You've got your bag filled with some stuff you'll need when your friend appears and asks you for a favor. *Could you please take this bodgit to my aunt? She lives where you're going.*

Huh? *What's a bodgit?* you ask. A bodgit is a thin, heavy silver object with hard bristles positioned every two inches. It's about a foot long and weighs about ten pounds. While it's not too big to bring along on your trip, it's pretty awkward. But you like your friend, and you owe them a favor, so you agree. Then you start to imagine what it might be like to travel with this thing. It's a bit on the heavy side, it won't fit in a pocket, and it's too uncomfortable to have it on your lap. Eventually, you find room to carry it in your bag. It goes with you in the car and, while it's a little awkward and heavy, it doesn't get in the way of your trip, and you deliver it successfully.

This bodgit represents uncertainty. In this example, you don't want it but you're willing to make room and bring it along because your friend matters to you, and the bodgit matters to them. When we think about uncertainty in this way, it becomes apparent that in order to live a life filled with people, experiences, and things that matter to us, we need to make room for uncertainty. And when we do this, the uncertainty doesn't actually interfere in, or disrupt, our lives the way we might expect.

MAKE IT COUNT!

Later on, in Tip 7, we'll help you discover a diverse range of things in your life that are important to you, the things that really matter the most in these four central categories:

- Relationships (friends, family, romance, others)

- Education, learning, work, and growth experiences

- Fun, recreation, sports, and music

- Personal growth, health, and wellness

For now, let's do this in brief. Thinking about these four areas, are there people, activities, or interests that are important or meaningful to you? We hope the answer is yes. But let's consider how uncertainty might also be part of these important people/activities/experiences. Do you always know how a friend feels about you or what your parent/boss/teacher thinks about you? Do you know how you will do on a test or how a game will turn out? Can you predict when you will get sick or whether something bad will happen at work/practice/school? For most of us, the answer is no, and this is because of uncertainty. We don't know what will happen tomorrow or next week, or whether things will turn out the way we want in any of the important areas in our lives. But just like carrying the annoying and awkward bodgit because it was important to your friend, so too can we learn to carry uncertainty with us regarding the people, activities, and pursuits that are important to us.

Accepting and making space for uncertainty is easier if it's for a purpose or cause. Pursuing the things that matter even with uncertainty present is that purpose and cause. In order to be our authentic selves when we are with the people we care about and when we engage in activities that count, we have to be willing to make space for uncertainty to come along with us on that path into the future. Take a brief pause and ask yourself: *Am I willing to make space for uncertainty in my life if it allows me to get closer to the people that matter and to engage more fully in my interests?*

LEMONS VS. LEMONADE

You've probably heard the expression, "When life gives you lemons, make lemonade." This advice suggests that when things aren't going the way you want, you can change them. This is true to an extent; you can change quite a lot, such as your hair color, clothing style, the causes you support, the words you choose, the foods you eat, your friends, how you behave, and much, much more. So that's the good news. But the bad news is that uncertainty isn't one of those things, and neither are feelings or thoughts. So when we're dealt lemons but cannot make lemonade, like when uncertainty strikes, there is some wisdom in accepting it as it is, and getting on with the rest of your day and life. Because the future hasn't happened yet, we will never be able to get rid of uncertainty. The only thing that's certain is uncertainty! That is the harsh truth, but we have confidence that you, like many of our clients, can learn to accept and live with uncertainty by *making space*.

CAUTION: ROUGH CONDITIONS AHEAD

By now, we hope you are opening up to the idea that uncertainty is unavoidable and that struggling against it is futile. Instead, we're offering you an alternative that involves allowing it to exist in your life. The paradox is that when you don't struggle with it (hint: Tip 2) and you make space for uncertainty, it causes less disruption and anxiety than when you try to control it or take steps to actively get rid of it. However, there are two conditions that can occur to challenge the ease of learning to make space: (1) when strong thoughts pop up or persist, and (2) when unpleasant sensations arise.

The Tyranny of Thinking

For many of us who struggle with uncertainty and, consequently, feel anxious, worried, or stressed, there may be specific thoughts that really grab our attention and escalate our feelings. They're *showstoppers*. They can be so real, mean, judgmental, or upsetting that we may find it's hard to make space for them. For example, these thoughts might say:

- *I'm unlovable!*

- *If (insert feared event) happens, I'll never have the life I want.*

- *If I touch that, I'll spread germs to others and they could die!*

- *I'll end up homeless and alone forever.*

- *It's my fault that (insert trauma) happened; I must be a bad person.*

- *This sensation feels different from before, and I think I'm dying.*

In other situations, clients report that it's not that they deal with particularly strong, judgmental, or loud thoughts, but they're just so darn persistent and they take up all the space. It's like they never shut up! For example:

- *They're probably mad at me.*

- *I'm gonna mess up!*

- *Something bad's gonna happen…*

- *I better be careful or I'll get sick.*

- *It'll be awful; I'll never be able to handle it.*

- *That's so unfair; it's just not right!*

Now, in the defense of our brain and the anxious thoughts it sends us, the brain is simply doing its job. As you learned in Tip 2, humans have the ability for complex thinking, which is intended to keep us safe. Our brains send us thoughts to protect us from perceived danger and to alert us to important things. But some of the time, those thoughts simply aren't useful and end up doing far more harm than good. Furthermore, some of these tyrannical thoughts may not even be true. Have you seen that bumper sticker *Don't Believe Everything You Think?* We love that one because it's true!

Scientists estimate our brains generate upward of six thousand thoughts in a single day (Tseng and Poppenk 2019), posing an important question: are all those thoughts meaningful? We're pretty sure the answer is no! It's simply not possible, and as a result, psychologists have developed techniques (outlined in the rest of this tip) to help clients notice that thoughts are just thoughts. They're words in our mind that come and go of their own free will. They're neither good nor bad—they're simply there. While some thoughts serve to protect us from danger, motivate us to meet our goals, problem solve, imagine, innovate, and more, at least a chunk of our thoughts serve no real purpose. If we can train ourselves to understand this, we will be less likely to overreact when uncertain and anxious thoughts pop up in our mind.

Severe Sensations

In addition to tyrannical thoughts, clients also report that sometimes when uncertainty looms, they feel a range of unpleasant bodily sensations that make it hard to focus or engage with routine demands, and making space for these seems out of the question. Examples include:

severe stomachache;

constricted or narrowed throat;

tight and tense back or shoulder muscles;

extreme fatigue or heaviness;

chest pain.

Do any of these types of thoughts (judgmental and/or persistent) or sensations ever happen to you? Start to pay attention over the next few days to any messages your brain sends you or sensations that arise when you are dealing with uncertainty, and write them down in a journal or on your phone. We're going to teach you some fun strategies that will make even the most serious person smile, but you'll need to use personal examples, so use your observation skills to start noticing what you think and feel when uncertainty strikes. As you'll discover, muddling the mind is a great strategy to navigate these rough conditions!

MUDDLING THE MIND

This skill is all about disrupting mental expectations—what we call "muddling." For most of us, our minds have trained us, and now expect us, to analyze every thought we have and to take every thought seriously. Unfortunately, this can cause more problems than it solves, so this skill is all about disrupting unhelpful patterns.

Chronic worry, fear, stress, and anxiety are serious psychological processes, and we certainly wouldn't want to minimize the disruption these can cause. In fact, in 2019, the World Health Organization did a study and found that depression and anxiety disorders cost the global economy $1 trillion (in US dollars) each year in lost productivity. However, despite the seriousness of this, humor can often be a wonderful anxiety disrupter. So rather than letting anxiety take center stage, we want to minimize its significance by using humor to disrupt the hold it can have over us.

Muddling the mind is a relatively simple three-part strategy (you can use any or all of these) that allows us to fundamentally change the relationship we have with our thoughts, urges, images, and sensations. Rather than getting caught up in whether these are true or meaningful, trying to get rid of them, or using other control strategies, we simply notice their presence, use a muddler, and move on. Muddlers are playful activities that help to reduce the power of our tyrannical thoughts and severe sensations. For example, when your brain sends you the zinger, *You're an embarrassment to your friends* (ouch!), instead of thinking more about this, recalling your past behaviors, and feeling ashamed or anxious, you start to play. We know it sounds like a strange idea, but it really works. Playing allows us to create space between ourselves and our fear of uncertainty, and as a result, the worry messages and sensations become smaller and a lot less threatening. We have created the following three muddler exercises based upon ideas from a host of excellent ACT clinicians (Harris 2019; Turrell and Bell 2016; Hayes and Ciarrochi 2015; Ciarrochi, Hayes, and Bailey 2012) and our hope is you find a few you like to use anytime a fear of uncertainty pops up.

Muddler 1: Playing with Words and Images

- **Sing.** Take your worry thought and try to sing them to the tune of a catchy song. How about Aretha Franklin's "Respect," except we can change it to your brain insult—*L-O-S-E-R-R-R, find out what it means to me (er, nothing!).* Or the ubiquitous "Happy Birthday," becomes *I'm such a lo-ser, no-bo-dy likes me, no-body likes me, it's true, I'm such a lo-ser.* As they keep singing their thoughts, most people find they just don't sting quite as much, and if you sing enough, you start to laugh at it all and not take them seriously.

- **Change your voice.** There are several free smartphone apps you can download that change the way your recorded voice sounds. Pick an app and simply record yourself saying your anxious or judgmental thought then play it back with a different voice. The more you hear it in a new voice, the sillier it tends to sound.

- **Flush it down the toilet.** It can help to imagine the individual words of your fear thought tumbling down the toilet like unwanted bodily waste, allowing you the satisfaction of flushing it away. Of course, like all thoughts, the message will return to replay in your mind; simply head back to the bathroom, imagine the letters and words falling into the toilet, and flush. And you have the backup option of washing your hands (for good hygiene too!) to remove any residual parts of that thought from you and wash them down the drain. Double wham!

- **Flick it off your shoulder.** A slightly gentler option to the toilet is the casual flick. Whenever you have a thought or image pop up in your brain, imagine it settling onto your shoulder, and then simply flick it off. This works well for less strong or mean thoughts or those thoughts that are pesky and persistent. Just keep flicking!

- **Scrub, swat, stomp, or smash it away.** When your thoughts are both strong *and* persistent, use actions with greater force. Wash the dishes while scrubbing away unwanted thoughts, or swat, stomp, or smash those intrusive thoughts and images with your feet and hands as you bake, walk, or play a sport. The thoughts may return within minutes or hours; if they do, simply repeat.

- **Play with your food.** Imagine the words are sitting in your mashed potatoes, sprinkled on your peas, or written in ketchup on your hot dog. Then take a good old bite, chew, and swallow, or mash the words into your food, and eat them up.

- **Hit an imaginary baseball.** Imagine the negative message as a ball of words in your hand, toss it into the air, and grab that imaginary baseball and *smack!* Make it a home run!

- **Use nature.** The next time you're outside, use what nature gives us and:

  imagine the words sitting in a rain puddle and jump up and down until the words are splashed away;

  let your thought float off in a beam of sunshine;

  allow the wind to pick up that thought and send it away on a breeze;

  pack your thought into snow and throw that snowball away.

The possibilities are infinite, so if you can think of a better or more appealing idea, go for it!

Muddler 2: Old vs. New Habits

Another strategy that can help is when we compare our old *way* of coping (steps 1 and 2 below) to this idea of making space (step 3). The next time you have a particularly strong or persistent thought, try doing each of the following three steps and then decide which of the options work best for you. (Hint: step 3!) Then use that option the next time you have tyrannical or persistent thoughts:

1. **Under the microscope.** Take your thought and analyze it. Put it under the microscope and really look at it. Ask yourself these questions and write your answers down if you choose to:

    Is this thought true? Think about all the data that makes it true. Consider that perhaps it's not true and recall all that data.

    What do other people think of it?

    Can I change this thought?

    Then notice how it felt to go through that process. Did it take up a lot of time and energy? Was it easy or hard?

2. **Fast ball.** Hit or throw that thought far away, and put all your attention and energy into keeping it far away. If it pops back into your mind, squeeze your eyes shut, and force that thought away. Don't let it back in. Turn your back on it. Use your hands and feet to push or kick it away. Run away from it. Do everything you possibly can to keep it away. Then notice how it felt to go through that process. Did it take up a lot of time and energy? Was it easy or hard?

3. **Air particles.** Imagine these thoughts, images, and urges as air particles that simply exist around you, like a fragrance or an aura. Sometimes there are many and sometimes there are few. You don't need to do anything about them; simply notice they are there and continue with the activities that matter to you. Allow them to be there without you having to engage with them. Now notice how this option felt. Did it take up a lot of time and energy? Was it easy or hard?

After trying each option, ask yourself these questions:

Which step was the easiest to do?

Which step took the least amount of energy?

Which step made me feel the least anxious or uncomfortable?

If you answered step 3 for all of them, you are right on par with the making-space strategy. Interestingly, many people find that when they simply let their anxious uncertainty thoughts exist without conscious effort to change, control, or eliminate them, the thoughts stop being quite as powerful. Please note that the strategies described in steps 1 and 2 probably send the opposite message to your brain than the third strategy does. Steps 1 and 2 make you either overanalyze the thoughts (and perhaps engage in rumination; remember AARS from Tip 2?) or expend a lot of energy trying to push the thought away.

In contrast, step 3 has you create space for the unhelpful thoughts or sensations while you focus your efforts on doing activities that matter to you, which naturally results in those thoughts or sensations drifting into the background.

Muddler 3: Softening Body Sensations

The next time your body experiences a strong or painful sensation, get your powerful imagination on the job. Send your attention inside your body and direct it to the sensation. Once you've arrived on location, try changing how it interacts with your body. If the sensation is hard, imagine it as soft. If there is pain with it, wrap the pain in a blanket to dull its impact or massage it until it no longer creates pain. The sensation is not gone (and that isn't the goal anyway), but you've used your imagination to change how it affects you. Or imagine the sensation as a distressed kitten and pick it up and soothe it until it no longer needs to get your attention by coming to you in the first place. Lastly, rub your hands together to generate warmth and then place them on the location, noticing how the warmth counteracts the intensity of the sensation. Even if the sensation remains, the warmth softens it, allowing you to focus on other important things in your life.

MAKE SPACE, NOT STRUGGLES!

We hope that you're starting to recognize that making space to coexist with uncertainty is a better option than continuing to struggle with it. As you will continue to discover, the tips throughout this book can help you live a less stressful and more authentic life even with uncertainty present. But before we proceed, we'd like to leave you with an interesting scientific study that highlights that disengaging from stress and anxiety (not necessarily intentionally distracting yourself) by focusing on something else can help reduce anxiety.

Researchers in Quebec studied 193 eighth-grade students with test anxiety and found that offering the students the option to either color freely or color a mandala image significantly reduced their anxiety prior to taking a test (Carsley and Heath 2018). What's interesting is that the students weren't directed to stop being anxious but were simply told to color. Perhaps by focusing on coloring, they were inadvertently allowing their anxiety to coexist alongside the activity. They made space for their anxiety while doing something that mattered (coloring). And the outcome? Their test anxiety decreased. Just imagine what might happen if every time you became overwhelmed by uncertainty, rather than struggling to control it, you could make space for it to be there and turn your attention toward something that mattered to you. What would your life look like? Would the quality of your life change?

TIP 4 TAKEAWAYS

In this tip, you learned the following:

- Recapping from earlier tips, uncertainty is everywhere, and the future is unknown, but this does not need to be a bad or dangerous thing.

- When you practice the making-space strategy for uncertainty (*observe, breathe, expand, allow*), things don't get worse and you can in fact tolerate the discomfort of uncertainty.

- Even if you don't always want uncertainty, being open and willing to make space for it means it doesn't have to interfere or disrupt your life—just like carrying a bodgit for a friend.

- Accepting and making space for uncertainty is made easier if it's for a purpose or cause such as pursuing the things that matter, even with uncertainty present.

- Although we all experience the tyranny of unpleasant and persistent thoughts, as well as challenging physical sensations, there are three awesome strategies (playing with words and images, using new instead of old habits, and softening body sensations) that can help you make space between yourself and those thoughts and sensations. This becomes a wonderful alternative to engaging and struggling with them.

This chapter's mission was to help you make space between you and the uncertainty you encounter in daily life by learning to coexist with uncertainty without it causing unnecessary stress, worry, and suffering. How able are you to create space in your life for uncertainty now?

1	2	3	4	5
not much		*some*		*a lot*

Giving Thanks to Uncertainty

This chapter's mission is to help you recognize and even develop an attitude of gratitude for what uncertainty has to offer you. How thankful are you for uncertainty?

1	2	3	4	5
not much		some		a lot

While our brains tend to magnify the negatives in our lives to protect us, as you've learned throughout Tips 1–4, 100 percent certainty is no longer a must to survive like it was in prehistoric times. Now, we can safely make space or even become frenemies with our unwanted anxious thoughts and feelings. Even though life is full of challenges and uncertainty, a strong body of research suggests that seeing the world through a gratitude lens, in other words, practicing being grateful daily, improves our overall well-being (Emmons and McCullough 2004; Emmons, Froh, and Rose 2019).

WEARING GRATITUDE GLASSES

Gratitude is an intentional appreciation for what we have or what someone did for us, big or small, tangible or intangible. Examples include being thankful for a beautiful sunny day, receiving a compliment from a teacher, having the support of a friend, and even learning from our mistakes. Intentionally seeing what's going well in our lives and connecting with things outside of ourselves, like other people, nature, higher forces, or spirituality, have countless benefits for our physical and mental health. For example, people who wear gratitude glasses, or are able to see the goodness in routine things, more often tend to have stronger immune systems and lower blood pressure. They also report feeling happier, more optimistic, and less anxious and depressed than individuals who show less gratitude. In addition, gratitude can improve sleep, relationships, learning, decision making, and even resiliency. In this tip, we will help you develop a grateful outlook on uncertainty. Building on the strategies from Tip 4 and making space for uncertainty, we will teach you additional strategies to incorporate gratitude into your routine and hopefully make life even more fun and fulfilling!

WHICH UNCERTAIN PATH TO TAKE?

When we think about uncertainty, most of the thoughts, feelings, and sensations associated with it tend to be negative. Not knowing or being able to control what will happen in the future can make us anxious, confused, and uncomfortable, regardless of the real probability of something bad happening. As a result, some of us may avoid uncertain situations to prevent these uncomfortable and unwanted feelings or engage in other ARRS actions discussed in Tip 2. At first, it can feel good when the uncertainty disappears and everything is seemingly back in our control. But is it? (Remember the uncertainty trap?) And how long can you go before uncertainty shows up again?

Ask yourself: *Do I give up anything when I avoid or remove all uncertainty?* For most of us, the answer is yes because we give up things that matter. For example, let's suppose you want to try a new club or sport at school. You think about joining something, but then don't because you realize you don't know who'll be there or if you'll like it or be good at it. As a result, you gain certainty about what your afternoon will look like, but you give up the possibilities. It could turn out to be an enjoyable new pursuit, or at worst, it's not for you but nothing bad happens. And if giving up things that matter isn't bad enough, there's more! When we avoid uncertainty, we have no opportunity to learn to deal with it, which means we remain feeling afraid and intolerant of it in the long run. We're stuck in the uncertainty trap!

However, as you learned in Tip 2, when faced with uncertain situations, we also have the option of choosing another path and getting out of the uncertainty trap. Traveling down this other path requires that we be open and curious about what uncertainty has to offer. In doing so, we have an opportunity to get outside our comfort zone and try something new, which we'll explore further in Tip 8.

When we take small, calculated risks, we have the chance to learn from our new experiences and even face the consequences related to uncertainty with more of a positive mindset. Using the above example, let's say that you signed up for that new club or sport, and none of your friends ended up being there. While being in this situation could suck in the short run because you feel like an outsider, you would have the chance to feel uncomfortable and attempt to connect with other students. Taking risks like introducing yourself to others or joining group activities, despite being anxiety-provoking, could actually improve your social skills and build your confidence. You would also have the opportunity to develop meaningful relationships and expand your social life. So, what does all this have to do with gratitude?

In dealing with uncertainty, gratitude doesn't come naturally at first because we don't really feel good in moments of uncertainty and tend to have a negative mindset. However, by intentionally noticing the good things even in challenging situations and seeing them as opportunities to learn and grow, we can improve our relationship with uncertainty. The first skill you will learn in this tip will help you appreciate both the positive and negative sides of uncertain things in life.

Skill #1: Two Sides of the Same Coin

Unfortunately, it's nearly impossible to experience only positive emotions and outcomes when we do things we care about. For example, suppose you value doing well in school. With that value comes hard work, stress, uncertainty, and at times, disappointment. Similarly, if you care a lot about a family member, you'll likely get hurt or mad when the two of you have arguments. In Tip 7, we'll dive deep into your values. But for now, we want you to remember that there are always two sides to every meaningful situation and the things we value in life: the challenging part and the good part. And without each part, we cannot have the whole experience. In other words, you have to be open to having the challenging side (even though it may not be so appealing) to experience and appreciate the good side. This is another example of *willing versus wanting,* which we discussed in Tip 4: we're asking you to be *willing* to accept the challenging side even if you don't *want* it.

To help you become aware of both sides and see the positives of challenging situations, we would like you to practice the following exercise. On your phone or in your journal, write down three things that are important to you right now. They could be related to relationships, school, work, or activities you do for fun or relaxation, health, or personal growth. Next to each item, write the good things about them that come to mind. After that, include the challenging stuff. Here are some examples of how to do this activity:

What's important to me	Good stuff	Challenging stuff
Exercising	Good for my health, I feel fit, I'm more relaxed afterward, I can better focus on homework.	Time-consuming, hard to schedule, got injured in the past, sometimes I don't feel like it.
Hanging out with friends	We laugh a lot, I can count on them, I don't feel alone, they keep me busy.	Friend drama, I worry about them, sometimes I don't feel I fit in.
Working	Money! Feeling independent, meeting new people.	Worry about being fired, less time for fun and to relax.

What did you notice? Is it possible to have only the good side of what's important to you without experiencing the challenging side? Probably not! So, when faced with uncertain situations, the formula is the same: being willing to take risks + feel discomfort = getting closer to what matters to you.

And having hurdles along the path (the challenges), such as making mistakes or feeling frustrated, is part of the process of getting us there. So, by taking risks regardless of the outcome, we build resilience and increase the chances of achieving goals that make life more fun and meaningful and being the person we want to be. Now that's something to be grateful for!

Skill #2: Gratitude Attitude

Now that you know that there are two sides to every situation, what can you appreciate when uncertainty pushes you outside your comfort zone? What does uncertainty bring to your life that you weren't aware of before? In this next skill, you will train your brain to see the unknown less as a burden and more as an opportunity to learn and grow. Before we dig into this concept, let's do a quick exercise using either your journal or phone.

List three valued activities that you've been avoiding because you fear the unknown outcome.

For each activity, write out the challenging thoughts, feelings, and sensations that will accompany the activity.

Next, identify the positives of facing the challenge if you were to wear gratitude glasses.

After completing this exercise, what is something in common that you noticed across these examples? Thoughts? Feelings? Body sensations? Maybe you realized that just the idea of diving into something new and unknown was stressful, anxiety-provoking, or frustrating. Yep, these are all shared experiences we as human beings have when dealing with the unknown.

How about the positives of going through these situations? What could you be thankful for? Maybe you noticed that by getting out of your comfort zone, you had the opportunity to learn something new (like how to bake a cake), become better at things (like relating to others), or accept help from others (when you don't know what to do on the first day of your new job). The more of these you do, the easier they will become. With practice facing challenges and having a gratitude attitude, your brain learns over time that you *can* tolerate and appreciate uncertainty. You accept the good parts and challenging parts and together see them as potential gifts rather than burdens. So, you come out of the experience with a deeper sense of appreciation for life. You have *gratitude*.

Skill #3: Gratitude Attitude in Action

Now that you know why gratitude is important, that everything in life has two sides, and that we can have a gratitude attitude, our next skill is to practice different ways of feeling and expressing gratitude. According to Dr. Robert Emmons, one of the leading researchers in this area, practicing gratitude involves two steps: First, we affirm that good things exist in the world as a whole, even though there are challenges, burdens, and disappointments. Second, we acknowledge that the sources of many good things are outside of ourselves, like in other people, higher powers, or spirituality. And in addition to these two steps, we also want to focus on being grateful for things that happened in the past, are happening in the present, and will happen in the future (Emmons 2007). We can focus on past experiences by remembering positive memories or being thankful for how things turned out after a struggle, or recalling what people did for us. We can also notice what's going well in the present or not take things for granted but appreciate them by noticing. Or we can be hopeful or optimistic about the future. Let's learn some ways of incorporating gratitude practice, or a gratitude attitude, into your daily routine.

Thanking the Past

Select a song on your phone or computer that makes you self-aware, sentimental, or reflective (often music with a calm or paced tempo works well). Before you turn it on, lie down on your bed or sit in a comfortable position with your journal or phone to take notes. When you're ready, turn on the music and listen to it for about thirty seconds to get in the mood. Now think about a past experience that was challenging and uncertain for you. As you think about it, notice how your body feels and the images or thoughts that come to your mind. Write them down. Next, look back at this experience and its outcome. Reflect on what you have gained from this experience. What's different about you? Do you see this situation in a different way now? What did you learn from it?

To enhance this skill, we encourage you to recall other examples in your life that you might have overlooked, and reflect on them. Consider using items you may still have lying around that help you remember the event, such as photos, ticket stubs, an award, or a memento. In addition to the uncomfortable stuff that happened, what else can you accept about the situation? What were the benefits of tolerating uncertainty?

Counting the Positives

Select a time every day—maybe when you go to bed at night—and write or mentally reflect about three to five positive things that happened to you during the day, big or small. Reflect on what went well or what you are grateful for. As you write or think about them, be specific and notice the sensations you feel while recalling these events. Make sure you count the positives of your day regularly and use a variety of examples rather than always being thankful for the same things. These items can range from the small to the large; for example, *Today I was grateful for the rain my garden needs, the warmth of my dog's snuggle, and the donut my friend shared with me at lunch.*

Visual Reminders of Goodness

Another way to help you remember to acknowledge the goodness in your daily life is to choose an object that can remind you of gratitude. This object could be a special rock, a painting, a photograph, or an elastic band on your wrist. Alternatively, you can set a phone notification to appear randomly throughout the day. Every time you see this object or the notification pops up, quickly name something positive that is happening in the moment. For example, if you're on your way home, look at the elastic band and identify what's good going on around you: *Is the sun finally shining after a rainy week? Will I be meeting my friend after school? Is there little homework to do today?* Whatever you notice as positive, give thanks to it.

Thanking the Present Struggle

In the next week, when you realize that you are struggling with uncertainty, like worrying, feeling stressed or stuck, stop for a minute and acknowledge what's going on (for example, by using CALM in Tip 2). Then think about the good stuff the situation can offer you by asking yourself:

What can I learn from this situation?

What would the people who care about me say to me in this situation?

What's something I recently learned from a challenging situation that can help me now?

What am I better at today to deal with this situation than I was last year?

Although this may feel unnatural at first, practicing this positive mental gratitude attitude in a moment of struggle can help you develop a more positive mindset to deal with it.

Thanking Someone

Being grateful and letting people know how much you appreciate having them in your life can improve relationships and increase well-being. There are different ways of doing this: in person; by text, email, or video; or writing a thank-you letter. Even thanking someone in your thoughts increases one's positive outlook in life.

No matter which way you choose to express your appreciation for that person's contributions to your life, make it a habit to thank someone a few times each month.

Mindful Gr-Attitude

Throughout Tips 1–4, you learned different ways to practice mindfulness. Mindful "gr-attitude" adds to this practice by encouraging you to intentionally focus on the present with a grateful attitude. This strategy involves using your senses in the moment without judgment to thank something or someone. This time, you will use your imagination and the sequence of steps you find most helpful for practicing the activity. Find a comfortable place to either sit or lie down. With your eyes closed, or open and softly focused on one spot, do the following (and if your mind wanders, bring it back gently):

- Take a deep breath and notice your surroundings, using your senses. What do you see, hear, and feel right now? Is there a smell or taste you notice?

- Take a few more deep breaths while noticing these sensations, then take a moment to think about an uncertain or stressful situation you recently experienced. Where were you? Who was there? What happened?

- As you bring such an event to your mind, notice how you feel in your body.

- Reflect about what was so challenging for you in this unknown situation.

- Try to recall what happened once you got through this situation. Was the outcome what you expected? If not, what was different about it?

- Looking back at this experience, in addition to the challenges you had (uncomfortable thoughts, feelings, or sensations), what did you learn from it? Was there something about this experience that you can be thankful for?

- The last step is to thank yourself for getting through this challenging event and learning from it. You can say to yourself something like, "Good job getting through this!," "You did it!," "It was hard but worth it." Use any words that make sense to you.

How did this exercise go? Is there anything about this experience that can help you deal with similar unknown situations that cross your path in the future? It would be great if you could practice mindful gr-attitude once a week.

Skill #4: Learning from Mistakes

As you've been learning throughout this tip, the uncertain challenges that show up in our lives can also be seen as opportunities to learn and grow, or be gifts we receive. Even professional athletes who seem to be near perfection in their sport, like basketball star Michael Jordan, acknowledge that they had to fail many, many times before succeeding. If you want to hear about this in his own words, type "Michael Jordan failure" into a search engine. You'll find a thirty-second video clip that highlights how he coped with missing nine thousand shots and losing three hundred games in his career, and yet these failures helped him succeed.

Can you think of a few times when you made mistakes and then became better at something or more mature, selective, or experienced because of it? Try to recall mistakes you made as a young child and as a teenager, perhaps when you were learning a new skill, participating in a competition, engaging in a relationship, or something else. What examples come to mind? When you reflect about them, what can you be grateful for and how did these mistakes make you grow?

Skill #5: Not Taking Things for Granted

As you've learned throughout this tip so far, the uncertain challenges that show up in our lives can also be seen as gifts; without them, it wouldn't be possible to experience the good side of things, and we wouldn't take risks, try new things, or learn from our mistakes. Facing struggles and appreciating them can make us stronger and wiser. Thus, it's important to make room for uncertainty (hint: go to Tip 4), treat it as a frenemy (hint: go to Tip 3), and be grateful for what it might have to offer (hint: this tip!). We would like to share with you Hayden's story about finding goodness during one of the most uncertain times of modern history, the COVID-19 pandemic. By practicing seeing the world through a gratitude lens, Hayden started to perceive uncertainty as an opportunity to grow and not take things for granted.

Meet Hayden

I'm Hayden (they/them). I live with my parents and have no siblings. I like spending time with my family, but prefer to hang out with my friends at school and on the weekends. While I never enjoyed most school subjects and have needed extra academic support since I was young, I loved participating in drama and band. Actually, it was much easier to get up in the morning and not be late to school when I knew I had those classes.

Everything changed when the pandemic hit and schools shut down for months. In the beginning, it felt like I was on vacation 24/7. Like I stayed home gaming all day long, talked to my friends online at any time, went to bed late, and woke up even later. At the same time, I felt bad knowing that so many people in the world were struggling with the illness and economic instability.

As the weeks passed by, the reality hit, and I started to get really sad and bored because I had nothing to talk about with my friends since we weren't doing anything new. I also began to miss seeing people for real—and even going to school! Online programming was not the same, and there was no more band or drama. Also, I felt suffocated by my parents, who were at home all the time and stressed out because they weren't sure about keeping their jobs. The uncertainty of not knowing about the future and when life would go back to normal was awful. I felt so sad that I even wondered if I was depressed. I talked to my friends about my feelings and found out that most of them were also feeling this way. I wasn't alone.

One day, while I was watching YouTube videos, one about gratitude popped up. I clicked on it and was surprised to learn that people who purposefully identify positive things that happen in their day, even if they seem insignificant, tend to feel better about life than those who don't. The video talked about training our brains to develop a positive mindset by noticing routine things such as eating a favorite food, going for a walk, or giving and accepting help. Then I watched a bunch more videos on gratitude and found some cool activities. My favorite one was to write a few things that I was grateful for in a gratitude journal every day. As I started to practice noticing the goodness in my routine, I realized that I was actually grateful for things that before the pandemic had seemed like a burden. For example, I noticed that I spent more quality time with my parents (despite sometimes feeling annoyed) when cooking meals, watching movies, or helping with the garden. With this extra time, I began to eat healthier and even learned how to cook a few vegan recipes. I now had the time to learn how to play the piano and was even becoming more confident at it. I also exercised more and spent time outdoors, enjoying nature as a way to see friends. Still, I missed my old life and realized I had taken some things for granted. Like being able to be physically close to people as we hung out in the halls between classes, going to a school basketball game, and even sitting in a regular classroom. Of course, I still would prefer life prepandemic, especially because fewer people in the world would have *suffered. But, despite the burden that the pandemic brought to everyone's lives, there was some goodness. I personally managed it well by eventually accepting life as it was, catching the good things, and reminding myself that I didn't have much control over so many other things.*

As you can see, Hayden had a hard time adjusting to life during the pandemic. Finding the goodness in such uncertain times was definitely not intuitive. However, with practice, Hayden trained their brain to wear gratitude glasses and see the good in things despite them not being easy or what they wanted. When you reflect on your experience during the COVID-19 pandemic, can you recall examples in your own life of things you took for granted prepandemic and then realized how grateful you were for them? What did you learn from having to tolerate uncertainty? In the next tip, we'll discuss why dealing with uncertainty is challenging and help you create a team of helpers to support you in coping with uncertainty.

TIP 5 TAKEAWAYS

In this tip, you learned the following:

- Acknowledging what's going well in our lives, even when things feel unsure and stressful, can lead us to positivity and more meaningful and fulfilling lives.

- Uncertainty can help us get outside our comfort zone, try something new, and learn from our experience.

- Every situation we value in life has two sides: the challenging and the good. Without one, we cannot have the other one, so we need to be willing to accept both sides of the coin to do things that matter to us.

- Gratitude practice is simple, and we can exercise wearing gratitude glasses every day. During uncertain times, such as the COVID-19 pandemic, we learn to tolerate uncertainty and be thankful for things we perhaps used to take for granted.

This chapter's mission was to help you recognize and even develop an attitude of gratitude for what uncertainty has to offer you. How thankful are you for uncertainty now?

1	2	3	4	5
not much		some		a lot

Understanding Social Uncertainty and Creating a Team of Helpers

This chapter's mission is to help you understand the value of social connections and discover how to identify and connect with people who can help you cope with uncertainty. How confident are you that you recognize the importance of social connections and have people who can help support you in coping with life's many uncertainties?

1	2	3	4	5
not much		*some*		*a lot*

As you learned throughout Tips 1–5, dealing with uncertainty is not an easy task. It all goes back to our caveperson's brains that perceived uncertainty as a threat to our survival because of the unpredictability of the outcomes we faced in routine life. Not knowing for sure if certain foods were poisonous or if that animal nearby would attack us could result in death. So, our brains adapted to alert our bodies (to feel uncomfortable) and minds (to generate protective thoughts) when uncertainty was present so that we could be ready for lifesaving action.

Fast-forward a few million years, and our brains continue to operate in the same way even though we rarely face life-threatening events in our daily lives.

Interestingly, as discussed in Tip 1, the degree to which each of us handles uncertainty can vary. Our own approach and willingness to take risks and get out of our comfort zone also influence how much uncertainty we feel we can handle. As you learned, some people are born more prone to have anxiety or have a harder time tolerating uncertainty because of genetics or a family history of similar difficulties (biology). Others may have experienced hardships or were taught to be overly safe, increasing their sensitivity to uncertainty (environment). And some people have a harder time taking risks because of personal characteristics such as being inhibited (shyness), seeing things as more dangerous than they might actually be, or having limited coping skills to deal with the unknown.

Although there is variability in how each of us tolerates uncertainty, struggling with it is a shared experience we can all relate to. Even those most tolerant of uncertainty can recall moments of wishing for more certainty. As a result, we can support one another when facing uncertainty, regardless of the level of felt intensity we individually experience. This is one of the main reasons we don't need to cope with uncertainty alone. In this tip, you'll learn the science behind human attachment and why we all crave social connections. You'll also discover (if you don't already know this!) the importance of creating a team of helpers and learn about the various types and levels of support they can provide you to improve your tolerance of uncertainty. Our goals in this tip are for you to get comfortable asking for help from the people who care about you and to support you in becoming a pro at tolerating uncertainty.

EARLY LIFE UNCERTAINTY

Believe it or not, our parents' love of us and ours of them stem from our need to live. Without a caregiver, many mammal species, including humans, wouldn't survive past the first few hours of life. So, nature has designed human infants to increase their chances of survival from birth on. For example, a fetus learns to recognize their mother's voice and scent to help them nurse within hours of birth (Sullivan et al. 2011). They are also born super cute and lovable to improve the odds of an adult (who may or may not be genetically related) wanting to stick around and take care of them. And being cared for is not just about food, clothing, and shelter. Infants, children, and teens need to feel that they are loved no matter what, that they are safe, and that they belong, all of which foster healthy emotional development, ensuring they grow up to be well-functioning adults (Harlow et al. 1959).

The bottom line is this: we are biologically preprogrammed to create attachments to our parents or caregivers not just to survive but to thrive (Bowlby 1977).

Interestingly, the need to stay close until one becomes fully independent and capable of survival also is present in many other animal species. For example, cheetah cubs need eighteen months of training in hunting before leaving their mother. Baby bears stay by their mother for about two and a half years before going off to hunt independently, while orangutans stick around for six to seven years to learn how to find food and discover what's safe to eat and how to build a sleeping nest.

And what about humans? In many westernized cultures, children may elect to stay close to their parents until their late teen years or into their twenties until they are ready to seek postsecondary education, gain steady and long-term employment, or marry. In cultures that share collectivistic values (versus individualistic values in westernized communities), parents may expect unmarried children to live at home (or nearby) until they marry, after which the adult child may still be expected to reside close by (Williams 2020). Regardless of our cultural background or age, when we leave home, staying attached to our nest is a natural part of being a social being. And science has identified that people with stronger social relationships (either from family connections or friendships) have a higher life expectancy (Hayes and Ciarrochi 2015).

SOCIAL UNCERTAINTY

In addition to the need for early attachment to their caregivers, back when our ancient ancestors were alive, survival depended on ensuring that we lived in groups. Because resources were scarce and danger was commonplace, if we were part of a group, our chances of survival were much higher than if we were left alone to fend for ourselves in the wild. This is because we could watch each other's backs (literally!), collaborate in hunting and fighting, and prevent our species' extinction by mating.

However, to belong to a group, we needed to be nice to be around, social, and have things in common with other cave dwellers. Think about it: What would happen if you took advantage of the food supply and relaxed in your cave all day long instead of helping out with hunting? Or if you did help out in the food department, but you were rude, annoying, or lazy compared to the other group members? Your cave buddies would probably kick you out of the group because you weren't contributing to everyone's welfare and, instead, were thinking only of yourself, reducing your chances of staying safe and alive for very long!

Now, fast-forward some millions of years to the present and reflect on how evolution has shaped our modern brains to socialize. Do you worry about fitting in? Being liked? Having friends? Belonging? If you answered yes to some or all of these questions, you're not alone. The vast majority of people worry, even if subconsciously, about being accepted by others. And they all experience a common discomfort when they feel unsure about whether they belong to a group. And, as you can see, this all originates back to the time of our ancient ancestors, when we actually needed to be part of a group to ensure we would survive. While our physical survival nowadays no longer depends on group connections, we still experience anxiety, sadness, and even anger when we are faced with social uncertainty. After all, we are wired to be social and to connect, to belong. But let's take a look at what can happen when we try too hard to belong.

UNCERTAIN PERFECTION

Our need to belong can help us be a good friend, compromise and work to fit in (especially in collectivistic cultures), and care about what others think or how we perceive ourselves in comparison to our own expectations. However, for some of us, our brains can push us to do these things to an extreme, leading to excessive worry and perfectionism. This means that some of us attempt to manage the uncertainty about not being good enough or meeting expectations by spending a lot of time and effort working really hard to get things "just right" or "perfect."

While striving for excellence can be adaptive and healthy because it pushes people to do better, it can also become problematic. It's one thing to set the bar realistically high to achieve high grades, perform well in sports, or be a trust-worthy friend. But it's another thing entirely to have over-the-top standards that are beyond reason and practically unachievable.

Occasionally, some people do manage to defy the odds and attain the almost unattainable. Unfortunately, their enjoyment of their success is typi-cally short-lived as they quickly move right on to the next challenge. When this happens, we set ourselves up for failure because, in reality, it's impossible to keep up with such high expectations 24/7, like only getting 100 percent on all tests or being the best athlete on the team or the most popular student in school to gain the love and respect of the people around us. Also, we end up perceiving mistakes as defeats rather than opportunities to learn and improve our skills. Our brain's default strategy becomes one of engaging in unreason-able self-criticism to push us to do better. And the results are not pleasant because we miss out on the fun and enjoyable life activities and experience high degrees of shame, anxiety, procrastination, avoidance, and even depres-sion. As you can tell, perfectionism can get in the way of life. Check out Jackson's story to see more examples of how perfectionism evolves over time.

Meet Jackson

My name is Jackson (they/them). For all my life, I dreamed about becoming a professional basketball player, so I've practiced basketball every day since I was little. I've always worked really hard and put a lot of pressure on myself because I worry that people will see me as a failure if I make mistakes.

Having high grades and being on the top basketball team have always been a must. To manage my expectations and feel more confident that I'll do well at school and score lots of shots at games, I spend all my free time studying for tests and practicing basketball. I rarely see my friends or hang out with my family. Overdoing things has worked out for me until recently because it gave me a sense of control.

However, last month, I started to feel overwhelmed with all the pressure I put on myself to have things perfect. I began to notice that even when I got an A on a test or someone complimented my performance after a game, my mind criticized me, saying that I could have done better or that others were just trying to be nice. I'm starting to get tired of this idea of perfection because there are days when I don't even feel like going to school or a basketball game. I'm also finding it hard to fall asleep and have no appetite, and I know good sleep and nutrition are key to playing well. I wonder if I'm depressed. Everything now feels like too much of an effort. I have a knot in my stomach most of the time, and I can't keep up with it all. I need to give myself a break!

Many other teens we work with, like Jackson, struggle with perfectionism. They're often high achievers who try to control their performance by working extra hard, yet end up feeling exhausted and defeated. So, even though perfection may reduce worries and increase certainty in the short run, it's not the best coping mechanism to deal with uncertainty in the long run. Therefore, if you struggle with perfectionism, we hope you are warming up to the idea of making space for uncertainty, and are willing to read the final three tips that will help you develop a plan for living a more meaningful and authentic life. But before we get ahead of ourselves, let's learn more about creating a social support team.

YOU ARE NOT ALONE!

So far in this tip, you learned that humans (and animals too) need to increase their chances of survival by developing strong early attachments to their caregivers and living in groups. You now understand that our fears of being different or not good enough are deeply rooted in our ancient ancestors' experiences and their need to survive.

Although the requirement to be part of the pack for survival is outdated and no longer necessary in the twenty-first century, feeling a sense of connection and belonging is. We can still greatly benefit from receiving support (not approval like back in the ancient days) from people who care about us to help us get through tough times. Thus, our mission is to help you identify and create a plan to connect with a social support team when you need that extra hand.

Research has shown that social support works in two ways: for protection and assistance. Social support can protect people from life stressors such as having a friend stand up for you if you are getting bullied. It can also assist us with tangible (like when you forgot lunch and have no money) or intangible help (like when you get emotional comfort from a friend after a breakup) (Langford et al. 1997). In fact, social support is thought to contribute to our psychological well-being by increasing a sense of control over our own experiences and reducing our negative expectations that bad things may happen in given situations.

SOCIAL SUPPORT COMES IN DIFFERENT SIZES AND FLAVORS

When you think about a social support group, do you think there would only be one member? Probably not, right? Just like an ice cream shop that offers a variety of sizes and flavors, social support comes in different levels and types. Sometimes we just need a small scoop, but other times we want to go for the ice cream sundae options, so it's important to have more than one person on your team who can provide more than one type of support. When you have a variety of people on your team, you may only need help from one person for small challenges, but for bigger issues, you can reach out to a bunch of helpers. As well, sometimes you just need one person for one moment, but at other times you might need that person or several people to be available for a week or longer. And if you have variety and one person isn't available, you have someone else to call on.

In addition to having multiple team members available for different sizes and lengths of the task at hand, it's important to be aware that different people can provide different types of support. For example, your parents might be a great choice to encourage you to join a new activity, like starting an art class or learning a new sport, and your teacher might be a good fit for helping you take risks when participating more in class discussions or volunteering to help out with a school event even if you feel like you won't get it right. Coaches can be great supporters of pushing yourself to new levels or taking on new challenges. And a close friend can be in charge of encouraging you to meet new people in your class or join a group during lunch break, or even just telling you that you're a great person worthy of meeting new people or trying new things. Even a neighbor could be a supporter in helping you apply for that new job at the grocery store near home or learn a new skill they already possess. The options are numerous! So, let's start to build your support team.

WHO IS ON YOUR TEAM?

As mentioned above, your support team could include all kinds of people ranging from family members to friends, neighbors, teachers, coaches, spiritual leaders, therapists or medical professionals, and more. Some of our clients have also included a pet on their team, and you can too, if you find that it may be helpful to have your pet to snuggle or to give you a reason to get out on a walk. Thinking about all these options, use your phone or journal to write down the names of people who are important to you in different life areas such as family/home, friends, school, community, sports/recreational activities, job/volunteer, religion/spirituality, and others.

What Type of Support Can They Provide?

According to research, social support also falls into four main categories: emotional, appraisal, informational, and instrumental (Langford et al. 1997). We'll share with you a few examples of what these types of support may look like so you can think of how each support team member can help you get through tough times:

- *Emotional support* is related to feeling heard and validated by others. These sources of support could vary from people you talk with deeply about your feelings to friends who can offer a lighthearted check-in. Some, including pets, may be helpful to provide comfort when you are stressed out.

- *Appraisal support* happens when we're reminded of our strengths and feel encouraged to try something or do better. Coaches are usually great at motivating us to continue playing when we're losing a game and therapists at helping us face scary situations.

- *Informational support* helps us resolve situations during times of stress. Support people like caregivers, friends, and teachers usually provide us with advice about solving problems like that argument you had with a classmate or how to study for that upcoming math test when you did poorly on the last one.

- *Instrumental support* is a concrete type of support usually provided by people who also give us emotional support such as a parent or relative who may help you buy a car or pay for college.

Given that different people can provide different types of support, next to the name of each person you listed above, add the type of support: emotional (e), appraisal (a), information (inf) or instrumental (ins), they can provide when you are having challenges with uncertainty. And remember, each person may be able to provide more than one type of support.

How to Connect?

There are different ways of connecting with your support team: in person; via phone, text, or video calls; and even in old-fashioned style, like a letter or package in the mail. How would you prefer to connect with each member of your support team? Think through how you usually interact or connect with each person and consider using that method. Then write this down next to that person's name.

Make a Plan!

Okay, now that you know who's on your support team, what type of help they can provide, and how you'll connect with them, let's make a plan about *how* they will support you. It can help to come up with specific scenarios or types of worry you experience, and then select a person and decide on the type of support you need. Keep in mind that you may need to come up with plans for several different areas of coping with stress and uncertainty. We've used Jackson's situation to illustrate this point:

Situation	Helper	Type of help	How to connect
Overstudying	*Close friend*	*(e) Listen and validate my worries about not doing well and help me set limits.*	*Video call*
Overpracticing basketball	*Coach*	*(a) Remind me that I'm a strong athlete and don't need to overpractice. Help me create a healthy basketball practice schedule and follow through with it.*	*In person (after practice)*
Eating and sleeping well	*Parent*	*(inf) Share information about the importance of sleeping and eating to improve my performance.*	*At home (during a quiet time)*
Seeing a therapist	*Grandparent*	*(ins) Help me pay for therapy sessions.*	*Phone*

Share Your Plan

Now that you selected your team members and thought about their role in supporting you, it's time to consider what you want to share, and with whom. For example, you may not want to share any performance insecurities with your coach but to simply ask and give them permission to push you to the next level. On the other hand, you may want to disclose to a close relative or friend that you struggle when things are uncertain and have clinical anxiety levels.

Then you could ask them to validate your feelings (emotional support) and encourage you to take risks (appraisal support).

As you learned in this book so far, avoidance and too much reassurance seeking, among other ARRS actions, are unhelpful shortcuts to deal with uncertainty (if you forgot how they are unhelpful, go back to Tip 2 and check out the information about automatic ARRS actions). If you know that these are actions you need to keep in check, explain and ask your helpers to call you on it when they notice you're avoiding things or asking for too much reassurance. Also, give them permission to encourage you to take risks even though they may be tempted to do the opposite!

Our last suggestion for this tip is for you to reflect and consider practicing what to say when you approach each member of your support team to ask for help. You could do this in writing, on a video chat or phone call, or in person. What you want to say and the language you'll use will vary depending on the person, but below is an example of how to approach an emotional supporter:

"Hey (helper's name), I've known you for so many years and feel like we can count on each other for anything. Because I trust you and you've been an important support person to me, I wanted to share with you that I've been struggling to deal with things when they're uncertain, and I feel worried, stressed, and anxious at times. These feelings sometimes get in the way of doing things that are important to me, so I've started to read about some strategies to cope with my worries. One of the strategies I learned is that I should ask people I care about to help me deal with uncertainty by taking risks and not avoiding. So, I wanted to ask for your support in continuing to be a great listener who gives me comfort when I need to vent about my worries. You always know what to say and how to make me feel better, even when there's no solution to what I've been going through. I'm very grateful for that."

To see how a team of helpers can support us, check out Asha's story about dealing with the uncertainty regarding what other people thought of her and getting help from the people who cared about her.

Meet Asha

My name's Asha (she/her). I've been shy for most of my life and have almost always cared too much about what others thought of me. My worries about being embarrassed or people not liking me were so big that I avoided doing things that most kids had fun with.

This all started when I was a child. I remember going into kindergarten and having a tough time staying at school for the whole day. I worried about not making friends, the teacher not liking me, and doing a bad job with my schoolwork. Because I felt so anxious and uncertain at school, I had lots of stomachaches and often went home early or was late for school. Outside of school, I also struggled to talk to people I didn't really know, like a cashier at a store, a restaurant waiter, or even my parents' friends. The worry about not knowing for sure if I was being judged or embarrassing myself kept me from doing things independently and socializing.

With the help of a therapist, I realized that many people in my life cared about me, and I could rely on them for support. My first step was to share some of my worries with my parents and grandparents and ask them to encourage me to try new things and talk to unfamiliar people when there was an appropriate opportunity. For example, when we went to a coffee shop or mall, they reminded me that I was strong and could take the lead and ask questions or pay for purchases by myself. I also made some good friends at school, but worried about being in group situations with other people I didn't feel comfortable with. So, my second step was to talk to two of my closest friends about how my mind constantly analyzed group situations and I feared that I'd embarrass myself. I told them that it really helped when they let me explain about my worries and, at the same time, pushed me a bit to interact with a few kids I didn't know very well.

I'm starting to realize that even if things feel uncertain, it's worth taking a chance because I'm strong and I have people to support me.

As you can see, Asha's fears of being judged and embarrassed kept her from meeting other teens, doing important everyday things, and especially being herself. Such fears about not being accepted by others are a shared experience rooted in the belief that not belonging to a group could result in death back in the day. But times have changed, and for some, social worries are not a big deal, whereas they hold others, like Asha, back from having a fulfilling life.

In this tip, you learned that you can ask for help to deal with uncertainty from people who care about you. How you'll approach different team players will vary, but now you have an idea of how to introduce your intent to get some extra help to cope with uncertainty. In the next tip, we'll dig deeper into your core values, or the things that matter to you, to boost your intention and determination to face uncertainty.

TIP 6 TAKEAWAYS

In this tip, you learned the following:

- Animals and humans are biologically preprogrammed to create attachments to their caregivers to protect them and ensure survival.

- Our fears of being different or not good enough are deeply rooted in the time of our ancient ancestors, when survival depended on ensuring that we belonged to groups.

- We all worry about not fitting in to some degree, but sometimes setting unrealistic standards can be unnecessarily painful.

- Receiving social support is essential and can be given by different people, in different sizes and flavors of help, ranging from emotional to appraisal to informational to instrumental.

- Your plan for building a team of helpers includes understanding the who, what, and, how of your team so they can support you in coping with uncertainty by using the strategies learned in this book.

This chapter's mission was to help you understand the value of social connections and discover how to identify and connect with people who can help you cope with uncertainty. How confident are you that you now recognize the importance of social connections and have people who can help support you in coping with life's many uncertainties?

1	2	3	4	5
not much		*some*		*a lot*

Pursuing Your Passions in the Presence of Uncertainty

This chapter's mission is to help you discover what really matters to you and learn how to pursue your passions even in the presence of uncertainty. How aware are you about the things that are important to you in life, and how much do you pursue them routinely?

1	2	3	4	5
not much		some		a lot

Although dictionary definitions vary, *value* can be defined as the importance, worth, or usefulness of something. So, by extension, values are the things that are important and worthwhile. We call values our *passions*, which are the "how" and "who" we want to be, the qualities we wish to display, and the actions and activities we do that matter most to us. The things we are passionate about may give us pleasure, a sense of purpose, or both. And engaging with our passions can allow us to feel a deep sense of fulfillment, meaning, and vitality, and serve to motivate, inspire, and guide us on our journey through life.

However, values are not something we can acquire or something that has a definitive end like a goal. For example, you cannot have a passion to be the president of a company or eliminate global warming. Instead, you can care about leadership, innovation, or discovery. Some examples of passions can include connecting (with others), learning (new things), giving (to others), exploring (uncharted locations), or being independent, loyal, open, honest, and much more. We'll explore more examples of passions later on in Skill #3, so if you're a bit confused, that's okay. As you keep reading this tip, all this information will start making sense to you.

PASSIONS ARE UNIVERSAL

Not surprisingly, the concept of a value or a passion is not unique to Western countries. It actually pops up in cultures throughout the world. For example, in Chinese, *chi* (or *qi*), means "life force or energy." Similarly, in India, *prana*, and in Polynesian countries, *mana*, are used to define a universal energy or life-giving force. And in Hebrew, *ruach*, and in Islamic countries, *barraka*, mean "life force." It's no coincidence that many communities throughout the world have a term that roughly translates to "living with purpose or a meaningful existence." Ultimately, when we live life with our passions as our guide, we tend to feel alive and have a purpose to be here on earth, even when things get challenging in the presence of uncertainty.

WHY PASSIONS MATTER

Before we help you discover and pursue your passions, we think it's wise to understand why doing what matters is important to a healthy and meaningful life. We considered summarizing some research demonstrating that following your passions can help you live longer, feel happier, and be less stressed. And while these studies exist—check out the *New York Times* 2018 article "Why Following Your Passions Is Good for You (and How to Get Started)"—we think it's more meaningful if you become the scientist-researcher and gather some of your own data to discover what happens when you follow your heart.

Take a few minutes to recall a day, or even just a few hours, when you last did something you really enjoyed, something that meant a lot to you. Perhaps you pursued your passion for music and played your guitar or listened to a new album. Or took the afternoon off and hung out with your friends or played a board game or watched a movie with your family, thereby pursuing meaningful relationships. Maybe you took the time to fill out an online petition for a cause that's important to you or volunteered your time or learned more about #Black Lives Matter or #MeToo events in your community to pursue your passion for social justice. If you cannot recall anything, set aside a few hours in the next week to do something that brings you pleasure or a sense of purpose and observe how you feel.

It's not important *what* you did (or do), but rather that you did something that mattered to you. With this example in mind, ask yourself: *Did it help me feel good?* And by *good*, we mean happier, less stressed, fulfilled, or purposeful. If the answer is yes, or even kind of yes, then we have data to support that passions matter in your own personal life.

Unfortunately, although the evidence is clear that living by your passions will lead to a fulfilling and healthy life, it's not that simple to make the switch. In fact, many teens we know struggle to put what they know into practice, especially when their lives are often filled with "have tos" like: "I have to get good grades," or "I have to help around the house," or "I have to look cool."

And although they understand that following their passions would be better for them, they end up being trapped in Zombieland.

TRAPPED IN ZOMBIELAND!

Zombie apocalypse is a genre of fiction most of us have either seen in movies or popular TV shows or read about in books. We bet you probably have some images running through your mind at this very moment: the not-so-human person stumbling forward, arms outstretched, dressed in ragged clothing, moving in mass with their fellow zombies, moaning, seeking to destroy any life force available in order to sustain themselves. And if you didn't have any images popping up, perhaps you do now! The central aspect of zombies is that they are devoid of life. They're trapped in limbo without a sense of purpose, unable to enjoy life, often unaware of their surroundings, following the crowd, and essentially barely existing.

Sometimes when we talk with our teen clients who are struggling with uncertainty, they share stories that have a similar flavor. They report feeling trapped in their daily lives and disconnected from what truly matters to them, mustering the energy to get to school on time each day, taking classes they don't always enjoy, not spending enough time with friends, having too many things to do, and feeling misunderstood and sometimes lost. Namid is like many of those teens.

Meet Namid

Hey, I'm Namid (he/they), and I love to learn about all things. I study hard because I want to become a doctor and help others. I'm really connected to my Indigenous Community and enjoy spending time with my family, friends, and community, cooking, connecting, and going to music events.

While much of the world became aware of the health disparities between dominant and nondominant groups as a result of the 2020 pandemic, I was already aware of this because of the historical oppression my ancestors experienced. This oppression is the reason I want to become a doctor, so I can integrate modern medicine with traditional healing practices (Two-Eyed Seeing).

But the further along in school I get, the harder it feels to pursue my passions, resulting in me doubting whether medicine is really the best path for me. I'm finding the academic demands both intense and sometimes irrelevant. And if that wasn't enough, I'm also struggling with the social pressure to fit into a certain "type." I often feel pulled in many directions trying to please my friends, family, teachers, and boss. All this has got me feeling lost, confused, and trapped in Zombieland.

Like Namid, sometimes when adolescents feel too overwhelmed, they stop doing things that matter to them and retreat into themselves. They may stop connecting as much with important people in their lives, withdraw from activities that used to bring pleasure, and start to feel numb, and even zombielike. Although we paint a bleak picture here, and perhaps this is not your situation in the first place, Tip 7 is all about stepping out of this raw painting and into something brighter, more hopeful, and truer to you.

ESSENTIAL SKILLS

We'll teach you four essential skills to fulfill this tip's mission: awakening, noticing, discovering, and pursuing passions. Let's get going!

Skill #1: Awakening

Even if you don't feel quite like a zombie, chances are, at least some of the time, you're operating on autopilot. We've all had those moments when we forgot where we put something, can't remember how we got to a place, or even missed what the other person said because our mind was miles away. Sometimes we reply with an automatic "I don't know" or "I'm fine," when in fact we're not. Although our minds cannot be 100 percent present 24/7, if we notice that we're spending a lot of time on autopilot and starting to feel down, stuck, or stressed, it might be time to wake up so we can live a more engaged and authentic life. Waking up involves using your five senses to start to notice your surroundings, which is similar to other mindfulness strategies such as CALM. (For a full review of this skill, go Tip 2). Take a moment right now to use your senses and notice:

five things you can see;

four things you can touch;

three things you can hear;

two things you can smell;

one thing you can taste.

Although you can do this exercise in less than a minute, it's not a race, and the more you spend time actually noticing what's going on around you and practice being awake and aware, the easier it will be to start living with your passions as your guide.

Some of our clients benefit from setting a goal to use awakening strategies for one to two weeks. They might set their alarm to sound several times a day as a prompt to pause for sixty seconds and be aware, using either the 5-4-3-2-1 awakening strategy or CALM exercises. The more aware we become, the more *awake* we are in life. And being awake is really the first step toward living a life filled with passions.

Skill #2: Noticing

As you begin to awaken and increase your awareness about yourself in the world, you can then start noticing some important things in preparation for discovering and pursuing your passions. As you know, uncertainty is every-where and is almost impossible to ignore. As you've been learning throughout this book, struggling against it is often futile. We've encouraged you to consider making friends with uncertainty, creating space, and even being grateful for when uncertainty shows up. There's a theme to all our recommendations: by letting uncertainty into your life, pursuing your passions becomes easier because you may recover from setbacks faster and continue to engage in things that matter.

So, let's take the noticing part of our brain and notice people in our communities who are good examples of pursuing what matters to them even when uncertainty exists. Do you know anyone who engages in an activity that challenges social norms or stereotypes? Dresses the way they want to even when others tease or bully them? States an opinion that differs from the mainstream? Keeps trying new things or sticking with an activity even when they make mistakes, fail, or aren't very good?

And if not in your community, there are excellent examples in the media. Check out these well-known people who pursued their passions when others said they shouldn't or couldn't. In doing so, they faced a very uncertain future, yet they kept going toward what mattered to them, doing the things they cared about and believed in. While reading their stories, try to guess who these people are.

Cut from the team: In tenth grade, he tried out for the varsity basketball team, but wasn't chosen. He was devastated and went home and cried. And then he picked himself up and got back on the court and played junior varsity like his life depended on it despite the ultimate uncertainty: *Will my hard work pay off? Will I make varsity next year?* And smaller uncertainties: *Will they laugh at me for not making varsity? Will they think less of me for my size* (he was five feet ten compared to many players six feet and taller), and *Maybe I'm not good enough to go pro.* He didn't let these uncertainties stop him, and he pursued his passion with steadfast determination.

Unfit for television news: Seven months after working as coanchor for a Baltimore news show, she was told she was "unfit for television news," an event that, in her words, "shook me to my very core." Whether this was because she was Black, a woman, or simply not yet skilled enough, it's hard to know, but perhaps it was for all three reasons. Having graduated from college and trained for this exact type of job, she suddenly faced the ultimate uncertainty: what now? However, she didn't let this uncertainty stop her, and instead she continued to pursue her passion in television and media with strength and courage.

Rejected from film school three times: He applied to the University of Southern California's film school and was rejected three times, resulting in his attending another college, only to drop out. But these experiences didn't deter him from pursuing his passions and directing and producing films. In fact, even when his career was established, he continued to face uncertainty year after year, as producers never know what the public will think of their film until it's released. Yet he continued to pursue his passions and is considered one of the greatest film directors, producers, and screenwriters of all time.

Wasn't chosen for the Olympics: She began figure skating at age eight and became a nationally competitive skater, but her career ended when she failed to qualify for the 1968 Olympics, a close call that devastated her but also propelled her to pursue a new passion: fashion. Although her anticipated career path was redirected, she poured her energies into another passion despite the inherent uncertainties this change created. Her willingness to keep trying despite the unknowns resulted in a massively successful fashion career.

If you didn't guess who these people are, here are the answers:

Cut from the team = **Michael Jordan** (Stibel 2017)

Unfit for television news = **Oprah Winfrey** (Ward 2017)

Rejected from film school three times = **Steven Spielberg** (Whyte 2021)

Wasn't chosen for the Olympics = **Vera Wang** (Olympic Channel 2020)

In addition to these people, there are an increasing number of athletes, musicians, actors and actresses, YouTubers, and celebrities who can inspire us with true stories of managing the uncertainty of *What will happen next? Will my fans still support me? Can this work?* and other unknowns they face daily.

A final example, which our colleague Rhye Paddack helped us put together, can be found in communities that *have* to persist in the face of uncertainty, not to just pursue their passions but to live their lives. Many adults in the transgender community do not begin the complicated process of gender transition until they feel established in their professional lives. This can happen for many reasons, an important one being possible job loss. The 2015 US Transgender Survey found one in six respondents reported losing a job because of their gender identity or expression. The same survey also found that over three-quarters of employed respondents said that they took steps to avoid workplace harassment, including hiding or delaying their transition or quitting their job. Despite the overwhelming uncertainty involved in the gender transition process, a 2021 Cornell University literature review found rates of regret around medical gender transition to be extremely rare, and in those cases, it was most often related to lack of social support or poor surgical outcomes related to surgeons using old techniques. This community provides excellent examples of making difficult decisions and not only making space for uncertainty but also acknowledging and embracing it to move forward.

The following people made many difficult decisions and faced enormous uncertainty before, during, and after their transition; yet being their full authentic selves meant making space for uncertainty in other parts of their lives.

Mauree Turner (she/they): As a Black Muslim American queer womxn in a conservative American state, Mauree experienced not being seen or heard by the people who made the laws in Oklahoma, where she lived. Despite this feeling of voicelessness and invisibility, they persisted and became the first publicly open nonbinary lawmaker in the country and the first Muslim state legislator in Oklahoma (Turner 2021).

Elliot Page (he/they): As a child actor, he wanted to keep his hair short and dress in a masculine way. However, his peers made fun of him because he was assigned female at birth, and casting staff asked him to wear wigs to present as more feminine. As Elliot became more established in their career, he could produce his own films and make a masculine wardrobe a condition of taking on roles. As time went on, he became more confident in expressing themself and came out as trans, instantly becoming one of the most famous trans masculine actors in Hollywood (Steinmetz 2021).

Kye Allums (he/him): His basketball career started to gain national attention when his high school basketball team ranked sixth in the USA Today Super 25 rankings. Kye continued on to the George Washington University basketball team and had a strong start as a player in the National Collegiate Athletics Association (NCAA). However, there had never been an openly trans athlete in the NCAA before, and prejudice against trans athletes in the country was only gaining momentum during Kye's basketball career. Despite not knowing how the NCAA and other athletes would treat him, Kye came out as trans in 2010 with the full support of his team and made history as the first trans athlete to play in the NCAA (Bleacher Report 2017).

Here are some other examples of trans community members who have faced incredible uncertainty and can serve as role models to have the courage to do what it takes to be one's authentic self: model Andreja Pejic; film directors/producers/writers Lana and Lily Wachowski; speedboat racer Hiromasa Ando; pop star Titica; golfer Mianne Bagger; actress and advocate Laverne Cox; and politician Georgina Beyer (The World from PRX n.d).

Noticing people who live their lives engaged in what really matters to them (whether it be their career or identity) despite uncertainty can help you prepare for doing the same. Over the next few weeks, look around you and notice friends, peers, family members, neighbors, and community members who offer examples of how to do this. Using your phone or journal, take the time to write down who they are, what you think they pursue, and what uncertainties they may face along on their paths forward. Consider whether their uncertainties stem from external factors like biases and job security, internal ones like self-doubt, or other reasons.

Skill #3: Discovering

As you, the expert on adolescence, well know, a pretty big part of being a teenager means discovering who you are. This means asking yourself some important (and sometimes difficult) questions like these:

- What type of a person am I? Kind? Funny? Smart? Athletic? Responsible? Musical? Creative? Loyal? Wise?

- Who do I want to be friends with, and what does it mean to be a good friend?

- What kind of a future do I want? One that involves thinking or analyzing? Doing? Creating? Exploring? Learning? Leading? Building? Fixing?

- When am I most myself? At home with a book? Out with a group of friends? Exploring nature? Playing sports? Being with my family? Protesting and advocating?

- How do my ethnic culture, heritage, gender, sexual orientation, economic standing, (dis)abilities, and religion/spirituality influence who I am?

As you can see, the answers may not come easily, and they can be complex and layered, just like traditional Russian matryoshka dolls, which consist of wooden dolls in decreasing size that fit inside one another. Our personality, or who we are, is typically layered with many parts of ourselves. While we do not expect you to suddenly discover yourself in this single, simple skill, examining your own personal passions can be the beginning of some meaningful exploration that will continue into early adulthood.

Teen of the Year

Let's imagine that you are being honored in a "Teen of the Year" celebration, and the emcee will share with the audience some highlights of your life. Think about what you would want this person to say about you. Before you continue reading, give yourself a few minutes to imagine...

What picture or story did your imagination create? It's probably not "(Insert your name) *loves skipping breakfast because they get up late for school and enjoys nodding off in science when they stay up too late cramming for a test. After school, they're grumpy to their parents and argue about chores before zoning out on their phone for the rest of the day.*" Instead, think about what you would want to hear the emcee share. Perhaps the emcee would honor you for your love of learning, kindness, loyalty, or confidence, or perhaps for your hard work, bravery, or openness. These would be your passions. The emcee may then go on to list the things you do to highlight your passions, which would be your pursuits, such as reading new books, listening to diverse music, taking a friend's urgent call at eleven p.m., spending Sunday afternoon with an ailing grandparent, and more. It's the actions you take each day that are your pursuits. While we know it's a reality that teens face many unpleasant demands each day and life is far from easy, you don't have to give up your passions and stop being your authentic self. And with a little attention and awareness to your daily habits, you can find smaller moments between these "have tos" when you can engage in your pursuits and be the Teen of the Year you really want to be.

Identifying Your Passions and Pursuits

Grab your phone or journal, and have it ready to use. We can organize the idea about who you are and who you want to be into four important areas of life:

- Relationships (friends, family, romance, others)

- Education, learning, work, and growth experiences

- Fun, recreation, sports, music

- Personal growth, health, and wellness

For each of these four areas, let's brainstorm potential ideas about (1) your passions: the things that matter to you or the qualities you wish to embody, and (2) your pursuits: the actions you plan to take to support your passions.

Using your phone or journal, create four sections to represent each of the four areas of life. Then divide each section into two equal parts (a T-chart). On one side, you will brainstorm your *passions,* and on the other side, you will list your intended *pursuits.* Keep in mind you may have more than one pursuit for each passion, and sometimes the same pursuit may apply to multiple passions. You can use any of the examples from the list below or come up with your own ideas. It's fun to use your own ideas, but if you get stuck, consider using an internet search where you will find lots of examples by typing "ACT values."

The following are some typical examples of the passions our teen clients have shared with us:

Adventure	Friendship	Openness
Assertiveness	Fun	Order
Bravery	Giving	Persistence
Caring	Gratitude	Respect
Connection	Honesty	Responsibility
Contribution	Humor	Safety
Cooperation	Independence	Sensuality
Creativity	Integrity	Skillfulness
Curiosity	Intimacy	Socializing
Exercise	Kindness	Supportiveness
Exploration	Learning	Trust
Excitement	Love	Willingness
Fairness	Loyalty	

Once you have identified your passions, you can start to think about the actions or pursuits you might take to support living your life with your passions in mind. The following are some of the passions and pursuits identified by Namid, who we met earlier in this tip.

My passions	My pursuits
Caring	Spending time with family and community
Connection	Hanging out with my friends
Contribution	Volunteering at the clinic
Curiosity	Reading about new things I've learned
Exploration	Researching universities
Fairness	Standing up for the rights of my community
Learning	Taking a new class
Persistence	Working hard in my AP biology class

Help! I'm Drawing a Blank

If this is the first time you've thought about what you feel passionate about and how to pursue these ideals, then it's not at all unusual to feel uncertain about your choices or be unsure how to start. As we mentioned earlier, we're not expecting you'll discover yourself in a single exercise. This skill can be developed over time, slowly, and with purposeful intention. This means that it's fine to leave your document empty and go do something else, but once in a while, give it a little thought. Ask yourself, *Have I done anything today that felt good, filled with me with purpose, or is something I'd like to do more of?* If so, chances are there's a hidden passion. And if your day has been filled with unpleasant demands, requirements, or has had you doing things you're *not* passionate about, then ask yourself, *What do I wish I was doing instead?* And then look at your answer to see what hidden passions might be revealed. (For example, if your pursuit was *I wish I was skiing,* your passion might be exercise or being outdoors.)

Stepping in Bubble Gum

Okay, now you know what your passions are, and you have ideas to pursue them, so off you go! Wait…not so quick, because just as you're starting to pursue your passions, you may be hit with a sudden burst of uncertainty, which is the metaphorical equivalent of stepping in bubble gum. Even if you haven't had the literal misfortune of stepping in bubble gum, you can imagine how it goes: Every step you take, your shoe gets slightly more stuck, making it harder to go forward. But if you stop to try and get the gum off, it starts sticking to everything and gets messier, slowing you down even more.

Stepping in bubble gum is a great metaphor for what happens when you start engaging with your passions only to get interrupted by uncertainty and doubt. When this happens, you may get sidetracked by uncertain thoughts and feelings that slow down your pace toward doing things that matter to you. For most of us, this is not an exception but the rule because uncertainty is a big part of our daily lives.

So, let's put some of these ideas into action. Suppose you really care about meeting new people and connecting with others at a deep level. You decide you'll join a new activity. As soon as you've made this commitment to yourself, uncertainty shows up. It speaks to you in a deep sinister voice, bellowing out: *People might laugh at the way you dress. They're probably way cooler/funnier/ smarter* (pick what your uncertainty would say) *than you.* You're suddenly doubting whether to pursue this activity, thinking *Maybe I don't need to meet new people.*

There it is…you've stepped in bubble gum! And you now have a choice: to notice the gum and keep moving toward this new activity, or to stop and try to clean yourself up and find a new path that's bubble gum–free. What do you do?

It is this scenario that many of us face daily, and the question is not so easy to answer. But to truly live by your passions and move toward what matters (in this example, to meet new people) you'll need to keep taking steps in the face of uncertainty. It's here that you can use some of the *SOS* and *making space* strategies from Tips 2 and 4, respectively. For example, you decide that you'd rather make friends than argue the pros and cons of joining a new activity (you drop the mental struggle), and instead you decide to make space for some uncertainty (you remind yourself there's space for uncertainty, trying something new, *and* that you can handle it). The net result: you sign up for the activity even though it feels a little uncomfortable. In addition, practicing some gratitude can really help. Like noticing that sometimes uncertainty's messages might even be correct (perhaps someone will be cooler/funnier/smarter than you), but that this doesn't need to stop you from pursuing your passions. In fact, you might become friends with that person and that's something to be grateful for!

In this example, you stepped in bubble gum, but kept moving toward your passions. And in doing so you noticed something interesting about the gum: it doesn't stay sticky forever. In fact, after a while, it gets hard and falls off, reminding us that stepping in gum doesn't have to slow us down.

Skill #4: Pursuing Your Passions—Gains and Losses

In addition to having strategies to get unstuck, it also helps to have a clear idea of what you stand to gain and lose when you pursue your passions in the face of uncertainty. If you expect there to be some uncertainty present at the outset, but understand your reasons for pursuing that path anyway, you can keep yourself oriented in the right direction even when uncertainty makes you doubt what you're about to do.

We (Juliana and Katherine) live in a rainy climate, and for ten months of the year, there's a good chance of rain. If rain stopped us from going out, we'd spend most of our days inside. So instead, we've learned to plan for it by carrying an umbrella, owning rain boots, and keeping a raincoat at work or in the car. And most of us find it's worth risking a little rain in pursuit of our daily plans. We can apply this same logic to pursuing your passions.

Let's begin with you thinking about a pursuit that is small and possible to do, but might not be easy because of uncertainty. Maybe you're passionate about honesty and you want to pursue this by sharing an opinion with a friend, telling your boss you cannot work an extra shift, or posting something personal on social media. Now think about what you'll gain and possibly lose when you pursue this action. Next, think about what you risk losing when you don't pursue this action because uncertainty has you convinced bad things will happen. Also, think about if there's anything you might gain. In this example, we might get the following:

Passion	Honesty	
Pursuit	*I tell my boss I cannot work the extra shift.*	
	Gains	**Losses**
I go for it	*I get the time off.*	*My boss might be mad at me.*
I get stuck	*My boss won't be mad at me if I push myself and end up working the extra shift.*	*I'm not being my real self. I miss out on my family BBQ and have to work instead.*

When we accept that there are no guarantees and the outcome is uncertain, taking the time to consider all the possibilities (good and bad) can give us the courage to step forward on our passion path and pursue the things that matter. Listing gains and losses is intended to help you live a more passionate life by understanding what's at stake, yet still pursue the activities that are important. We will walk you through how to do this in more detail in the next tip, where we look at how to pursue activities and goals that typically cause worry and anxiety for many teens.

A FINAL WORD

One of our favorite quotes is from Audre Lorde, a self-described Black, lesbian, mother, warrior, and poet who writes: "There is no such thing as a single-issue struggle because we do not live single-issue lives." Her quote reminds us that adolescence is a time of complexity, with layers of challenges to encounter. For this reason, discovering your authentic passions and learning to pursue them is critical. We hope that this tip and Tip 8 will provide you the courage, strategies, and pathway to find your direction.

TIP 7 TAKEAWAYS

In this tip, you learned the following:

- Our passions are the things we value and are a universal experience for all people. Passions include the "how" and "who" we want to be, the qualities we wish to display, and the things that matter most to us.

- Passions are vital to our existence, helping us live longer, feel happier, and be less stressed even in the presence of uncertainty.

- Sometimes teens can feel trapped in their daily lives, disconnected from what truly matters to them, causing them to forget to live with their passions in mind, and to retreat into themselves, feeling numb and even zombielike.

- Being trapped in Zombieland happens to lots of teens, and these four important skills can help you exit: awakening, noticing, discovering, and pursuing passions.

- Watch out for bubble gum (aka uncertainty)! Uncertainty can cause us to feel stuck and step away from pursuing our passions. Fortunately, we can learn to adjust and recognize that stepping in gum doesn't have to slow us down.

This chapter's mission was to help you discover what really matters to you and to learn how to pursue your passions even in the presence of uncertainty. How aware are you about the things that are important to you in life and how much do you pursue them routinely now?

1	2	3	4	5
not much		*some*		*a lot*

Taking GRASP Risks

This chapter's mission is to help you take concrete action to face uncertainty. How likely are you to take physical steps toward the unknown?

1	2	3	4	5
not much		*some*		*a lot*

In the last tip, you became aware of the things in life that really matter to you. Knowing and reminding ourselves about our passions when faced with uncertainty can help us get through difficult situations. It can also motivate us to experience uncomfortable thoughts and feelings in the service of something bigger. This tip is a very important one because it contains the most research-supported ingredient to help you manage your anxiety, fear, and worry during difficult times: facing the unknown. It has two main aims: (1) to help you understand the importance of taking valued-guided actions in face of uncertainty, and (2) to help you develop and implement a plan to do this. After reading this tip, we hope that you will be even more likely to take action when uncertainty tries to stop you.

CLIFF JUMPING

Have you ever been to the edge of a cliff? Imagine that you went on a hike with your buddies to try to find an amazing hidden waterfall. Friends of friends have been there and posted incredible pictures of this waterfall on social media. You were told that the hike was tough but worth the effort, so you and your friends go on a mission to find the waterfall. After hiking for an hour through a very steep and rugged trail, you get to the end of the path, where there's a cliff. You were told that if you jump off the cliff and swim toward the mountains for about five hundred meters, you will get to the secret spot. What do you do?

First of all, you look down and see the beautiful turquoise water at the bottom. Then you realize that the waterfall also seems pretty high, much higher than you first anticipated. As you think about this, you notice your muscles tensing up, your heart beating fast, and your hands getting sweaty. You can't really control your body's natural reactions at all. One of your friends who is not afraid of heights tells you, "Don't be scared!" And as they just say these words, your body reacts and your fear of heights begins to grow instead of shrink. Even though you try hard to stop these feelings and body sensations, it just doesn't work.

Then another buddy who notices your stress level tries to help and says, "Don't focus on the height!" Guess what happens next? As you attempt to suppress the thoughts of the cliff being high, just like you did with the *scratch your head* experiment from Tip 3, your thoughts about the cliff being too high increase exponentially. As a result, your mind begins to replay all kinds of worst-case scenarios that could happen if you jumped. These include landing on your butt and getting hurt, the water being too shallow at the bottom and, after jumping, getting lost and being stuck in this place forever.

Finally, another friend suggests you take a few steps back and do some jumping jacks. Are you able to move your body like that, despite feeling scared and having unhelpful thoughts? You probably can. As silly as it feels, you move away from the edge and do some jumping jacks, and you think about how much you want to see that waterfall and remember the things that matter to you in life. You notice your friends have taken the jump and are calling your name, so you quickly decide to go for it. You run toward the cliff and jump. The fall is fast, and once you hit the water, you get a rush of adrenaline and feel so proud of yourself. Even though you were scared and had unhelpful thoughts about the fall, you did it! And it wasn't as bad as your mind had been telling you...

Reflecting on the scenario above, what did you have control over: (1) your thoughts, (2) your feelings, or (3) your actions?

If you chose option 3, you are correct! What we *do* with our bodies, or the *actions* we take, like taking a few steps back, doing jumping jacks, or jumping (or not jumping) off the cliff, are the only things we can actually control. As you learned in the previous tips, it's nearly impossible to stop unhelpful thoughts and feelings. Despite your brain's automatic reactions to try to distract from or avoid discomfort, you now have the tools to leave such thoughts and feelings in the background rather than letting them guide your actions. (If you're unsure about how to do this, return to Tip 4.) The more you commit to act in the service of your values and passions, the more likely uncomfortable thoughts and feelings will become background noise. This is how a camera lens works: when you focus in on something, the surrounding content becomes fuzzy and out of focus. Your eye needs to see only what's really important; the rest does not have to be in focus because it doesn't matter.

TRANSFORMING PASSIONS INTO ACTIONS

To pursue our passions, as described in Tip 7, or to get to that beautiful waterfall, we often need to put ourselves in uncomfortable situations that don't feel great in the moment but are worth it in the long run. For example, even if you worry about talking to new people (fear), you still volunteer for that job to get signatures for a petition (take action) because you care about the earth (passion). Or if you aren't sure about how your friends will react to your new look (fear), you still dye your hair purple (take action) because you love looking stylish (passion). What researchers call "committed" action involves knowing what matters to us and heading in that direction by pursuing it. In order to get good at pursuing your passions, you're going to learn how to take GRASP risks, which are **g**radual, **r**epeated, **a**chievable, **s**urprising, and **p**assion-driven experiments. By taking GRASP risks, you'll learn that you can stand uncertainty and anxiety fairly well and get closer to what matters to you. In the next section, we will describe the science behind the benefits of taking risks. You'll discover that challenging yourself by taking action is the most effective way to reach your passions and teach your brain that you can do it.

UNDELETABLE MEMORIES

Before we dig into the specifics of GRASP risks, we want to give you some background about how memories can influence our behavior. To do that, let us take you on a quick tour of the brain. When we're exposed to events or situations in our environment that are meaningful or repeated over time, our brain creates memories about these experiences that are often hard to forget. These could be positive experiences such as going on a trip or receiving an award, or negative experiences like having a bad argument with a loved one, being bullied, or failing a test.

Because our brain cannot store all the information we absorb from the environment, some memories are thrown away. Not forgetting something important is useful if that something benefits you; for example, remembering a chemical formula before a test. However, sometimes our brain also stores memories that are unpleasant or unhelpful and plays them on repeat, like remembering wiping out at the skate park and everyone laughing at you. Understanding how memories are formed and realizing that we're unable to delete them are relevant for becoming motivated to face our fears and deal with the unknown. Let's use an example to highlight this idea.

Imagine that you're very scared of spiders. You don't really have a reason to be scared as nothing bad has happened to you, but your brain tells you that all spiders are ugly and dangerous, bite, and of course, can kill you. So, one day, you're in your room on a video call with a friend and see something moving on the corner of your bed. You don't even have enough time to process the information that that thing is a spider when your *amygdala* (the bean-shaped part of your brain that deals with fear and other emotions) automatically sends a message to your body to get ready to survive. In a split second, you start screaming and run out of your room. What happened here?

Well, your brain perceived the spider as something uncertain and potentially life-threatening because it connected this thing you saw in real life (the spider) with your prior learning and memories that labeled the spider as bad and dangerous. This connection triggered a fear response and prepared your body to act in a way that would ensure your survival; that is, to run away. Unfortunately, because you ran away and didn't test out if the spider would actually bite you, your memory that spiders are dangerous became even stronger and harder to forget. So, the next time you see another spider, your reaction will probably be somewhat similar (if not bigger). Fortunately, even though we cannot delete unhelpful or fear-related memories, new research has figured a way out of this cycle. Believe it or not, the solution to dealing with old and unhelpful memories that contain the uncertainty of long-standing fears is by actually building new memories *and* pursuing our passions.

NEW MEMORY BUILDER

In psychology, researchers and scientists are continually working to improve old theories as well as discovering new ones to help us live longer and more healthy lives. One such theory developed by Dr. Michelle Craske and colleagues is called inhibitory learning theory (Craske et al. 2014). It states that while we cannot delete or change original memories associated with fear (for example, spiders = danger), we can create new memories about similar situations with revised associations (for example, spiders = not all bite). These revised associations don't delete the old ones, but they serve as new associations that are stronger and more dominant, which means that you'll remember them better than the old ones.

For example, let's say that you embarrassed yourself at a party, and someone took a picture of it and posted it on social media. You feel terrible and now you associate parties with embarrassment and know that this picture will exist somewhere on the internet forever. However, you decide to take GRASP risks and end up attending a bunch of social events in a row and don't embarrass yourself. Your friends also post pictures of you having a great time. Because you have a lot of positive new memories of these social events (for example, many pictures), even though you didn't delete the embarrassing one, you no longer see parties as threatening.

The cool thing about this theory is that it gives us the power to change our relationship with the things that make us scared by allowing us to take GRASP risks and test out whether our feared outcome happens. Instead of avoiding uncertainty or playing it safe, we can begin to face our fears and create new memories with revised and more helpful associations and do things that matter to us. Let's meet Beham, who decided to take GRASP risks and live a more meaningful and fulfilling life despite uncertainty.

Meet Beham

My name is Beham (they/them). I'm a shy eleventh-grade student. I've always struggled to talk to other kids. Even though I like the idea of hanging out with people at school and would love to have more friends, I really have a hard time initiating conversation and keeping up with other students' interests while we're talking. When I push myself to talk to a few people in the class, I feel exhausted when I get home at the end of the day. Since the beginning of the year, the uncertainty of not knowing if people like me or if I'll embarrass myself if I cannot keep up with the conversation has held me back from sitting with other students during lunch, staying at school after hours, and even participating in class.

I started to see a therapist who pushed me to get out of my comfort zone and take risks to socialize. During our sessions, I realized that friendships and especially having a romantic relationship are really important to me. I also noticed that because I've been avoiding socializing for so long, my chances of meeting people are now very slim because I'm out of practice. I learned that avoidance has only made the memory that I might embarrass myself if I talk to people stronger, which ironically keeps me avoiding even more. I also discovered that I can't really delete this memory from my brain. The only way out is to put myself in anxiety-provoking social situations with the goal of talking to others and see what happens. By doing that, my brain will hopefully create new and more realistic memories about socializing. To do that, my therapist and I developed my GRASP risks plan and set a specific timeframe to complete my daily challenges.

WHAT GOES INTO A GRASP RISKS PLAN

As previously described, GRASP risks involve gradual, repeated, achievable, surprising, and passion-driven experiments that will create new memories that you can handle anxiety and distress and do things that matter. In the next sections, we will guide you through these five main components. As we explain what each letter of the plan means, try to relate that to your own experience.

GRASP: Gradual Goals

Dealing with the unknown requires us to tolerate uncertainty and engage in situations that may feel risky, scary, or temporarily uncomfortable. Therefore, being thoughtful and developing a concrete and gradual action plan about the kind of challenges you're ready to try is essential. The goal is to work your way up little by little (from practicing easier experiments to harder ones). For example, let's say that you're afraid of being late for school and wake up super early because you need to leave thirty minutes before school starts, even though it takes only five minutes to get there. However, being rested and doing well in school is also important to you. You may want to start a challenge by leaving home twenty-five minutes before the bell rings on the first two days, then twenty minutes, then fifteen…all the way until you're leaving home just five or ten minutes before school starts. There's no rule of thumb about how quickly you need to work your way up to reach your goal, so maybe you adjust your target time weekly, not daily. This adjustment may depend on your level of readiness to take risks and may vary depending on the situation or the people involved.

GRASP: Repeated So It Sticks!

Like trying to build muscles by going to the gym only once, facing a fear of spiders only once wouldn't be enough to create a new and strong memory that not all spiders are dangerous. Our brain needs repetition, tons of repetition, that gets reinforced over time when we intentionally put ourselves in diverse and uncertain situations for extensive periods to see what happens. Returning to our spider example, uncertain situations could include going camping and sleeping in a tent where spiders might be present, having a picnic and watching spiders crawling through the grass, or cleaning spiderwebs in your basement. As you imagine yourself taking these risks, and doing them not just once or twice but often and repeatedly, how would you feel and what would you think about? Probably anxiety and unhelpful thoughts would show up. So why would you do it? Even though there's more than one answer to this question, what the research tells us is that when we put ourselves in uncertain situations repeatedly and take risks, we learn something new and create a new memory that may become stronger than the (fear-related) old memory. And, consequently, this new memory can help motivate us to stop avoiding and start engaging in our passions, which in this case might be hanging out with friends, camping, and going on picnics.

GRASP: Achievable and Realistic

Make sure that the challenge is achievable and realistic. An achievable risk should make you feel challenged enough, but not so much so that it becomes unattainable. For example, don't expect that you'll be 100 percent accurate and make no mistakes at all during your presentation. Or that people will look at you at all times and ask a million questions to show interest. Instead, make space for minor mistakes to occur while you're carrying it out such as allowing people to drift off from time to time. Also, the risk needs to be realistic given your available time, commitment, and resources. For example, if you aren't using slides or reading from a script while presenting, don't expect to know every single detail of the content you present. It's okay to forget a few things or not know the answer to some questions.

GRASP: With a Surprise Effect

When dealing with uncertainty, our brain typically predicts that the outcomes will be negative to an extreme, and that we will be completely unable to cope. Interestingly, the key to building new memories is *not* to prove that the fear is unreasonable or that you will no longer feel stressed or worried. We cannot guarantee that because there are situations when the fear is valid or you will feel worried.

Instead, the aim of taking GRASP risks is to allow new learning by noticing the mismatch between what your brain expects will happen (for example, "All spiders bite," "I can't handle them") and what happens in reality (for example, "I didn't get bitten this time," "The feeling was manageable"). This is what we call the surprise effect. The bigger the surprise (or gap) between what was predicted and what occurred, the stronger the new memory about handling scary things will be. For example, if you stay in the room with the spider, you could learn, that for those ten minutes, the spider didn't bite you. Or if you cleaned the basement and a spider climbed on your shirt, you learned that you didn't die this time.

Your brain ends up creating a new memory (not all spiders bite) that inhibits the old memory (all spiders bite). If this happens repeatedly, your brain realizes that anxiety-provoking stimuli are generally safe, temporary, and manageable (Arch and Abramowitz 2015). So next time you encounter a spider, your brain retrieves the nondanger associations of all the challenges you put yourself through, and you will be more likely to take risks and engage in meaningful and fun activities that you hadn't previously been able to.

GRASP: Passion-driven

It is important to remember that we cannot guarantee that negative outcomes won't occur. Similarly, we cannot promise that your anxiety or discomfort will completely drop when you take risks. As we mentioned before, the key ingredient of taking GRASP risks is to *learn something new* or *gain new knowledge* from the experiment that provides evidence to your brain that you can handle distress and do things that matter despite experiencing discomfort. In other words, the number one reason to take GRASP risks is to get you closer to pursuing your passions, not to be certain about the outcomes or to be free from anxiety. No pain, no gain!

Your GRASP Risks Plan

Now that you have enough information about the musts of a GRASP risks plan, it's time for you to create your own on your phone or journal:

Step 1. Select up to three fears or uncertain situations, and reflect on what you want to learn or gain from facing these challenges and why. Below are some examples of what teens typically share with us when we ask them about their fears, but you can pick anything that is relevant to your life:

Fear/Focus	Passion	Pursuit/Importance	Learning goal/ New memory	Behavioral experiments
Doing things imperfectly and making mistakes	Having fun	Spending less time on schoolwork so I have time to do two or three fun things every week	It's okay to make mistakes, and I can handle the feeling.	1. Write an assignment with messy handwriting 2. Double-check my work only once. 3. Give a presentation and make a small mistake on purpose.
Failing a test	Achievement	Trying my best in school, but not aiming for perfection; being okay with some Bs	I can study as much as other students do and get a mark above 70 percent.	1. Spend no more than two hours a day studying. 2. Go over the study materials no more than three times. 3. Go to bed no later than ten p.m. even if I didn't finish studying.
Talking to new people	Friendships	Expanding my social circle and getting to know people who are different from me	I can keep up with a conversation with unfamiliar people for at least five minutes, and even up to fifteen.	1. Say hi to a student I don't know in my class. 2. Join in a conversation when I don't know all the people. 3. Introduce myself and ask two questions of another student in my class.

Having a panic attack	Adventure	Traveling and visiting new places	I can go to places and not have a heart attack.	1. Go to a coffee shop and order a drink. 2. Go to the mall and walk around by myself. 3. Explore a new park with my parents.
Giving my opinion	Genuineness/ Truthfulness	Being true to myself and standing up for what I believe	I can express my opinion to my friends, and they won't contradict every single point I make.	1. Post something personal/ important on social media and don't delete it. 2. Have a conversation with my best friend on a topic we don't agree about. 3. Purposefully disagree with a friend during a discussion.

Step 2. Think about what you want to pursue and describe it in a concrete and realistic way. For example, if you have a hard time going to school and are always late, perhaps the end goal is to be at school on time every day.

Step 3. It's important to create a list of challenges from easy to hard and work your way up (the G in GRASP). We encourage you to develop from five to eight different experiments about the same challenge (for example, getting to school on time once a week, then twice a week, and so on). The pace at which you move your way up will depend on how ready you feel for the next step. Sometimes you may find the challenge you were practicing too easy or boring, or you may just feel motivated to try something harder. It's up to you.

Step 4. Now that you have a list of experiments to practice facing uncertainty, it's time to put them into action. It'll be helpful if you schedule a time to practice the challenge every day; otherwise, you may forget or take longer to reach the goal. Remember that repetition is key—just like going to the gym once a week won't get you results nearly as fast as going once a day.

Step 5. Keep these questions in mind as you practice the experiment:

Before I take the risk: What's my goal? What am I worried about the most that will happen? And on a scale of 0–100, how likely is this to happen?

After I take the risk: Did the things I was worried about happen? How do I know? What did I learn from this experiment?

Step 6. Once you've implemented the plan, track your progress. One way of doing it is to answer the questions in Step 5 before and after practicing the experiment. Another way is to use a difficulty scale from 0 to 10 (0 = easy peasy; 10 = super hard) to rate how hard you thought the challenge would be before attempting it and then how hard it was in reality after you did it. When this first challenge is no longer a challenge, it's time to create another action plan following the same steps.

We hope you enjoyed learning more about the importance of taking risks and teaching your brain that you can face uncertainty despite not being fond of the feelings and thoughts that accompany it because you really want to do things that matter to you. In the next tip, you'll learn strategies to be kind to yourself when you make mistakes or go through something hard.

TIP 8 TAKEAWAYS

In this tip, you learned the following:

- We cannot control our thoughts, feelings, or sensations, but we can control what we do with our bodies by taking action to teach our brain that we can deal with uncertainty.

- While it's not possible to delete unpleasant or fear-based memories, we can create new ones by taking GRASP risks, seeing what happens, and doing what matters to us.

- GRASP risks involve creating experiments that are gradual, repeated, achievable, surprising, and passion-driven.

- The goal is to gain new knowledge from the experiment that provides evidence to your brain that you can handle distress and do things that matter despite what your brain thinks or how your body feels.

- It's key to practice GRASP risks frequently and monitor your progress when facing new challenges.

This chapter's mission was to help you take concrete action to face uncertainty. How likely are you to take physical steps toward the unknown now?

1	2	3	4	5
not much		*some*		*a lot*

TIP 9

Being Kind to Yourself

This chapter's mission is to help you be kind to yourself when you have a hard time dealing with uncertainty, failure, or disappointment. How likely are you to treat yourself kindly in challenging moments?

1	2	3	4	5
not much		*some*		*a lot*

Throughout the tips in the book, you've learned that our minds are hardwired to produce unhelpful thoughts, and our bodies react in uncomfortable ways. This happens automatically to help protect us from harm when faced with the unknown. You've also learned and practiced a range of strategies to get comfortable when dealing with uncertainty.

But even when we're doing our very best, sometimes things don't go exactly according to plan. When this happens, we may feel like failures and notice our minds beating ourselves up. This negative internal dialogue that often says something like "You need to do better!" "You're not good enough!" or "You messed up!" intends to push us to do better, but it doesn't. Instead, it spirals us down a self-criticism route that takes us away from reaching our passion-driven pursuits. Because all minds sometimes engage in self-defeating talk, in this tip, you'll learn ways to be kinder to yourself when you notice your mind being nasty to you. We hope that by the end of this tip, you'll have helpful strategies to treat yourself with kindness and compassion in life's challenging moments.

JUDGY MINDS CALL FOR KIND ACTS

Being a teenager is not easy! In addition to all of life's demands, teens go through significant physical and psychological changes throughout adolescence that can be challenging and exhausting. These changes range from maturing bodies, brain development, and hormone fluctuations to a need for more independence from your family and a quest to find your own identity. When faced with general life difficulties, failure, or a sense of being inadequate, our minds may become very judgmental and harsh toward ourselves. This is because our brains have the false belief that self-criticism can push us to work harder and overcome failure when, in fact, it goes in the opposite direction.

For example, imagine that you worked really hard on a group presentation for school. When it was your turn to present, you froze and forgot what you were going to say. It took you a few seconds to recover, but still, you ended up sharing only half the material you had prepared, due to anxiety. As a result, your group got a lower mark than you all deserved. You feel embarrassed and think of yourself as a failure, which is only made worse when your classmates tell you how bad you are at presenting and say that they don't want to work with you again.

How would you feel in this situation? Probably awful, right? Do you think such comments would help you prepare and do better next time you had a group project? Possibly, but likely not if you end up feeling so bad about yourself that it causes you to not spend your time trying and caring, or even to give up.

Now, imagine a different outcome after the group presentation. When your group received a low mark, one of your classmates said, "I know you worked really hard and got nervous when you had to speak in front of the class. We all get stressed out with public speaking. Next time, we can rehearse the presentation together and maybe practice presenting it to a smaller group before the whole class. We enjoy working with you and know you can do it."

How would you feel this time? Maybe still not great, but less embarrassed and more hopeful? And which scenario would be more likely to help you succeed at a group presentation next time? We're sure you can tell!

As you can see with these examples, the students in the first scenario made mean and judgy comments. In contrast, the classmates in the second scenario were more understanding and optimistic while not ignoring the problem of you getting anxious and not delivering the presentation as expected. They also acknowledged your mistake and suggested alternatives for you to do better next time, while being supportive and relating to how you felt.

We understand that you cannot control what others say, but our point is that how we're treated affects how we feel, which in turn impacts what we do. If classmates talking kindly to us results in longer-term benefits than when they're mean, wouldn't it be better to apply this same logic to ourselves when that inner monologue starts talking to us?

Using the examples above, think about how you'd treat yourself if you messed up in such a situation. If you're like most of us, beating yourself up would be the rule, not the exception. However, scientific research in the growing field of self-compassion tells us that in moments of emotional or physical pain or suffering, going in the opposite direction of self-criticism, like being more supportive and gentler to ourselves, has incredible and long-lasting powers for our well-being.

WHAT'S SELF-COMPASSION AFTER ALL?

The term "self-compassion" was coined by Dr. Kristin Neff, an outstanding psychologist and researcher (Neff 2003). Dr. Neff defined self-compassion as being kind and understanding to ourselves when faced with failure, disappointment, or a sense of inadequacy. For example, not getting that mark you expected after studying a lot for a test, getting yelled at by a parent, or messing up when speaking with your crush at school can bring up lots of judgy thoughts that are often hard on us. While we can't really control our thoughts and feelings, we can talk to ourselves in a gentle and nice way. Learning how to be kinder to ourselves can help us deal with uncertainty and manage our nasty minds in more productive ways. This is the essence of self-compassion.

Believe it or not, research has shown that people who are kind to themselves still set the bar high, but aren't as disappointed when they don't reach their goals. When faced with failure, rather than dwelling on negative feelings and thoughts, they actually come up with new goals (Neff and Davidson 2016). For example, if you bombed your driving test three times in a row, rather than getting stuck in the *I'm a failure!* thought, you come up with alternatives to do better next time, like practicing driving on new routes and parking in tighter spots. Research has also shown that self-compassionate people have an internal desire to learn and grow rather than a need to impress themselves and others. This means that if, for example, you aren't the best soccer player on your team, instead of trying to prove that you're the best, you take this opportunity to learn from more skilled teammates. Other characteristics of self-compassionate people include stepping back, acknowledging and taking responsibility for their mistakes with more balanced feelings, and accepting how they feel in that moment with kindness out of a place of growth and curiosity rather than fear or disappointment.

FROM THEORY TO PRACTICE

A key thing to know is that self-compassion has three main components that can be put into practice: mindfulness, common humanity, and self-kindness.

Mindfulness refers to the act of bringing awareness to a struggle without judgment. Rather than ignoring or exaggerating the challenge, we give ourselves permission to have those uncomfortable thoughts and feelings while leaving harsh comments in the background.

Common humanity is the part that reminds us that we're all human beings who are allowed to suffer and make mistakes. When we understand that if we didn't suffer or mess up from time to time, we'd probably not be human, we also normalize our struggles and see them as a shared human experience.

Self-kindness refers to the part of acting toward ourselves in a gentle and understanding manner, as opposed to being critical or judgmental.

Skill #1: The Self-Compassion Break

Dr. Neff has developed an awesome exercise called the *self-compassion break,* which is a brief and effective tool to use when uncertainty, disappointment, or self-criticism show up (Neff 2015). Read the steps first and then use this strategy any time you feel like you're struggling with internal self-defeating thoughts or shameful feelings.

Think of a situation in your life that is hard or stressful. Try not to select the hardest challenge you face, but something that is moderately difficult. Focus on it until you can notice the thoughts, images, feelings, memories, and sensations about this situation.

Next, tell yourself one of the following sentences to acknowledge this present struggle:

*This is a tough/stressful/difficult/*_____ (or insert something more specific) *moment for me.*

Aargh, this hurts!

Here's anxiety.

This sucks!

You can also use your own words to say something that suits your situation.

Remind yourself that it's okay to feel this way by saying the following words:

Having a difficult/tough/stressful/_____ (or insert something more specific) time is a part of life.

Other people would feel the same way in my situation.

I'm not alone.

It's okay to fail. I'm a human being!

Again, you can use your own word to say something else that suits your situation.

Next, make a caring gesture. Some people like to place a hand over their heart or on another part of the body that feels comforting, or even give themselves a hug. Find something that feels supportive to you.

Finally, end the practice by saying to yourself something that will bring *kindness:*

Let me be kind to myself.

I am strong.

I can handle this!

I forgive myself.

I can be patient.

…or anything that suits your situation. For example, ask yourself, *What do I need to hear right now to show kindness to myself?*

What are your thoughts about this exercise? Do you think it could help you take the power away from your mind's nasty comments when you're struggling? We'd like to encourage you to read this exercise again and come up with your own script using your own language. You may wish to write it down in your phone notes or your journal.

In summary, it might look something like this:

I'm dealing with this situation.

It's really hard on me and I'm struggling.

But I know other people have dealt with this or similar things, so I know I'm not alone.

With my hand on my heart, I tell myself, "I've got this. I can cope."

After recording this, please practice it once or twice to get the hang of it, and then use it any time you believe it'll be helpful. Next, we'll teach you three more strategies to strengthen your self-compassion toolbox.

Skill #2: My Kind and Younger Self

We have adapted the heart of this skill from ACT practitioners Dr. Sheri Turrell and Mary Bell, who in turn adapted it from a mediation they learned from Dr. Kelly Wilson (Turrell and Bell 2016). And because it has now gone through various changes, we encourage you to use the parts of this skill you like, but to modify it to suit your own needs and personalize it. The concept behind this skill is to get in touch with your younger (part 1) *and* older (part 2) selves—the person you once were and the person you have yet to become— and in doing so, to tap into an inner kindness that you possess to guide you through the uncertain times in your life. Here's how it goes:

Part 1:

1.   Start by getting into a comfortable position where you will not be distracted or interrupted. As you settle into this moment, take some slow deep breaths, and try to recall an image of your younger self when you first noticed struggling with the things you struggle with presently. For example, if you have a mean inner voice that tells you you're not good enough, you messed it up, or others don't like you, try to recall an earlier time in your life when that voice first spoke up.

2.   Pay attention to that younger version of yourself. Notice where you are, what you're wearing, your body posture, facial expression, and more. As you look at your younger self, notice how they may be feeling. Are they lonely and scared, or perhaps, rejected and sad? Move toward younger you and put your arm around them or hug them, and share some kind words such as, "I know this is hard, but I'm here to help," or, "I get it and you're not alone."

3.   Spend some time connecting with younger you and being there with no judgment and an open heart. Let younger you know that you will watch over them from now on, and then ask them to settle inside you so that you can continue to walk together through the difficult times.

4.   Once younger you is settled within you, pause and take a few deep breaths, and notice how you feel.

At this point, we hope you will be feeling softer and calmer, but if you remain anxious or tense that's okay, as there is a second part to this skill. Now that you have connected with younger you, we want to direct you to meet older you. For some of our clients, meeting their younger self is enough. If that's the case for you, you can skip over the remainder of this practice.

Part 2:

1. If you would like to be supported by your older self, take a few deep breaths and imagine yourself in the future. Look at your older self who has followed your passions and achieved the pursuits and dreams. Again, notice where you are, what you're wearing, your body posture, facial expression, and more. As you look at your older self, notice how they may be feeling. Are they happy? Confident? Strong? Notice how they possess qualities you admire and watch as they come over to you and sit alongside you.

2. Listen as they tell you, "I know you're struggling and life is hard right now. But you will get through this, and I'm here to guide and support you in this journey." Let them hug you, and as they do, feel the warmth and strength they're giving you.

3. Notice how you feel loved and supported. When you're ready, invite them to enter you and fit within your body, to be present with you from this day forward.

4. As you end this mental moment, take a few deep breaths and allow older you to settle into your body alongside younger you, and to be an invisible source of kindness and strength.

Treating yourself in a kind and supportive manner, as you'd do if you were your younger or older self, can help you recover from setbacks much faster than you can imagine!

Skill #3: Being Your Inner BFF

Another strategy to increase your self-compassion skills is to become your inner BFF. The principle is similar to channeling younger you; however, this time, you'd imagine helping a good friend who was going through something hard. These steps will guide you through this exercise:

1. Imagine that your good friend is going through a tough time and you want to help.

2. What would you say and do to support your friend? What words would you use? What would be your tone of voice?

3. Remember a time when you were going through something difficult. How did you talk to yourself? What was your intonation? Were you judgmental? Harsh? Mean at all?

4. Now compare how you'd talk to your friend to how you speak to yourself in moments of struggle.

What's the difference? You probably noticed that you were much kinder and supportive to a friend than to yourself. So, your next challenge is to practice treating yourself as you'd treat your friend in a similar situation.

Skill #4: Acts of Loving-Kindness

Now that you know some self-talk strategies to be compassionate to yourself in moments of suffering, we'd like to teach you one more strategy that focuses on compassionate actions. Research and our clinical and personal experiences tell us that being kind to ourselves, to close family and friends, or even to strangers can improve our well-being. In fact, practicing acts of kindness has been shown to increase our energy level, sense of happiness and pleasure, biochemicals that make us feel good, and even life span! Furthermore, acting with kindness lowers our blood pressure, pain and stress levels, and anxiety and depression symptoms (Hamilton 2017; Rowland and Curry 2019).

A cool study conducted in twenty-four countries divided adults into three groups: Group 1 was asked to do at least one act of kindness daily for a week toward people they were close to, like friends and family. Group 2 was asked to act kindly toward people they were less close to, like acquaintances and colleagues. And Group 3 was asked to do kind acts toward themselves. Kind acts included helping a neighbor, writing a thank-you card, going for a walk, or meditating, among many other things. The researchers found that, compared to a group who didn't try to be kind at all, acting kindly in all three groups *equally* increased the happiness of the person performing these acts. And this happened no matter to whom these acts were directed (Rowland and Curry 2019)!

The take-home message from this study is that being kind to others or to ourselves has many, many benefits, so we should come up with a game plan to help you practice kindness daily.

Please take a look at the list that follows. Select from five to eight kind things that you can start practicing or doing more, either for yourself or others. You can also add ideas of your own:

Go for a walk

Do a physical activity; for example, dancing, swimming, or biking

Get a good night's sleep

Eat a healthy meal

Listen to a favorite song or album

Take a break when feeling overwhelmed

Enjoy a favorite food

Bake your favorite dessert

Take a bubble bath

Sing at the top of your lungs

Go for a drive

Shoot hoops or pucks

Watch the sun rise or set

Declutter your bedroom if it has been bugging you

Read a book

Try out a new hobby

Donate time to charity

Cheer someone up

Help someone with work

Say no to someone you've had a hard time setting boundaries with

Do something to improve the environment (collect garbage on your street, walk instead of driving, bring a reusable mug to your fave coffee shop)

Text/video chat a friend

Edit who you follow on social media

Do something fun with family

Visit someone you haven't seen in a while

Give a compliment

Write a list of ten things you're grateful for and why

Now that you've selected several kind things to do, the aim is to practice at least one kind act each day for a week and notice the effect that acting kindly has on you. It's possible that once you start being kinder to yourself or to others, acts of kindness will become automatic. Or that you'll notice opportunities to practice kindness that you never realized before.

TIP 9 TAKEAWAYS

In this tip, you learned the following:

- When faced with general life difficulties, failure, or a sense of being inadequate, our minds can be judgmental or harsh to ourselves with the false hope that this will help us do better next time.

- Instead of beating ourselves up, practicing self-compassion strategies is a more effective way to help us deal with self-criticism in moments of suffering.

- You can use the self-compassion break exercise, listen to younger you offering you some support, or think of how you would talk to a friend in challenging times.

- Acts of loving-kindness toward ourselves, others close to us, or even strangers can improve our well-being. We just need to do them regularly!

This chapter's mission was to help you be kind to yourself when you have a hard time dealing with uncertainty, failure, or disappointment. How likely are you to treat yourself kindly in challenging moments now?

1	2	3	4	5
not much		some		a lot

Looking Ahead to Life with Uncertainty

This chapter's mission is to help you prepare for the next year and beyond by pulling together all your new knowledge and putting it into action. How prepared do you feel to apply your new knowledge to live your life fully even when uncertainty shows up?

1	*2*	*3*	*4*	*5*
A little		*some*		*very much*

You've made it to the last tip of the book! Well done. By now, you're an expert in managing life's many uncertainties. So rather than risk overloading you with more, this tip is designed to summarize what you have already learned and help you apply this new knowledge to your daily life, even when things get bumpy.

IT'S A WRAP!

We're hoping that you're (almost) ready to accept that life is full of uncertainty, and that learning to cope with curveballs is more useful than trying to control everything around you. One main skill you'll learn in this final tip is planning for what lies ahead over the next twelve months, which can help you embrace the ultimate uncertainty: your future.

As we wrap up your learning from this book, it's a good time to look at the main themes and skills you gained throughout Tips 1–9. The following list outlines the main points and one main skill you practiced from each tip that supports why you're ready to be comfortable with uncertainty. And if you get a little overwhelmed as you read this list, that's okay. We felt the same way reading over everything we had taught you! If you can't remember it all, you can always go back to each tip and look through the full chapter. This is just a summary.

Tip 1: Certainty was once fundamental to keeping our ancient ancestors alive, and although some of us still crave it more than others, we don't need it to survive in modern life. In fact, teens are in a unique position to cope well with uncertainty because they encounter it so frequently throughout adolescence. The main skill you got from this tip was *knowledge acquisition,* when you learned all about the science behind anxiety and our human desire for certainty.

Tip 2: Life is full of struggles, so rather than fighting against unwanted anxious thoughts, feelings, and urges, it's healthier (and easier) to drop the struggle and learn to coexist with life's many uncertainties. One skill you learned in this tip was the *SOS,* which highlighted the importance of stepping out of the struggle to find certainty in all you do by slowing down, observing what's going on around you, and then shifting into a meaningful activity.

Tip 3: Anxiety and uncertainty don't have special powers. In fact, many of the things we fear never come true. Our brains are well-designed to help us through stressful uncertainty, so rather than our seeing it as the enemy, uncertainty may have some things to teach us. One skill you learned in this tip was *from magnify to minimize: shrinking worries,* which taught us that our fear of uncertainty can magnify the significance of events when in reality they're mini in size, and we can cope.

Tip 4: Being open and willing to make space for uncertainty, even if you don't always want it, doesn't have to disrupt your life. Ironically, creating space between you and your anxious thoughts and feelings leads to decreased anxiety. The main skill you learned was *muddling the mind*, which offered you various playful activities to change your relationship with your thoughts from one of control to one of acceptance—and even fun!

Tip 5: Giving thanks to uncertainty can help us appreciate some hidden gifts uncertainty may have to offer. One main skill from this tip was *gr-attitude*, where you learned a variety of ways to look at your experiences and appreciate all they have to offer.

Tip 6: Social connections are essential to our survival, and wanting to fit in is normal. Harnessing the care and support of important people in your life can help you learn to live with life's many uncertainties. The main skill you got from this tip was learning how to *create a support team.*

Tip 7: Discovering what really matters to you, your passions, and learning how to pursue these even in the presence of uncertainty will give your life purpose and direction. The main skill you got from this tip was *discovering passions and pursuits,* which helped guide you in identifying your passions and making discrete plans for how to pursue those passions in your daily actions.

Tip 8: Having a GRASP plan to face uncertainty and pursue the passions you identified in Tip 7 can help build confidence and remove the spotlight from anxiety. While memories cannot be deleted, we can create new ones. The main skill you got from this tip was learning how to set up *GRASP* experiments that are gradual, repeated, achievable/realistic, surprising, and passion-driven.

Tip 9: Being kind and compassionate to yourself is more effective than engaging in a harsh inner dialogue to get through life's most uncertain moments. In this tip, you learned how to select and engage in daily *acts of kindness.*

MY LIFE, MY WAY

Now that you've done a brief review of the key points of each tip and the skills that you've learned throughout this book, we'd like you to do a similar review of your passions and pursuits discovered in Tips 7 and 8. Take a few minutes to skim back over those tips or look at the notes you took in your journal or phone to help you recall what really matters and the actions you might want to take to pursue those passions. Or right now, quickly jot down three things that matter to you in each of these four areas:

- Relationships

- School and work

- Personal growth, health, and wellness

- Leisure and recreation activities

As we go through the rest of this tip, try to keep these in mind and remember that living a full and meaningful life where you pursue these passions means accepting uncertainty.

WHEN YOUR PATH GETS BUMPY

Now that you have a clearer picture of what matters to you, your passions, and have learned in Tip 8 how to GRASP these important pursuits, you'll need to be prepared to do this even when things get difficult. It will come as no surprise to you that life is full of bumps and unexpected hurdles. But if you can expect the unexpected, you'll find that the inherent uncertainty in pursuing your passions becomes a source of strength rather than of weakness. The strength arises from the gains you acquire in pursuing your passions when you don't let uncertainty talk you out of it. For example, imagine you have a passion for environmental justice, and you join a teen environmental group even though you struggle with social anxiety. Joining this team means you will face lots of uncertainty, but it also means opportunities to take care of the earth and make new friends. This can lead to an increase in confidence and inner strength.

In the next section, we'll guide you in how to prepare for some of what lies ahead on your path during the next twelve months. This does not mean you'll always know what to expect, nor will it remove all uncertainty. For example, you might expect to play basketball, but your season performance remains unknown, or you know your course schedule, but there is no guarantee or certainty about the grades you'll get. In fact, in some situations, the only thing that's certain is uncertainty!

Before we look ahead, we need to learn about two types of bumpy road conditions.

Potholes and Sinkholes

The key to coping with an uncertain future is to have a plan to *get comfortable with uncertainty* just as the book title suggests. This means, in addition to knowing which skills will help you the most and being ready to use them, you'll also want to be able to predict events when and where you can. (We'll discuss this in the following section). But even with a plan, there are some bumpy road conditions to consider.

As you proceed on your uncertain life journey, you'll need to watch out for *potholes*, which are annoying dips in the road that are generally benign and don't stop your journey, and *sinkholes*, which can swallow up the whole car so that the journey ends abruptly! These two types of road bumps are metaphors for the impact that anxiety and uncertainty can have on your journey ahead. In the first case (potholes), anxiety and uncertainty are irritants and cause a minor delay on your journey, but you can get back on track when you use your skills or seek some support from friends, family, or a counselor. But in the second example (sinkholes), anxiety and uncertainty stage an attack and force you off the road. In these situations, the skills in this book may be insufficient to help you carry on, and when teens report sinkhole levels of anxiety and uncertainty, it generally means it's time to get professional help. The following are examples of each type:

Potholes	Sinkholes
Anxiety that lasts for a few days or a week at the most	Anxiety that lasts weeks and doesn't seem to improve
Having up to three panic attacks over the course of a month (when you previously had them daily)	Having daily panic attacks with no end in sight
Declining an invitation to a social event, but still going to a few others	Declining all social invitations and staying home
Having a couple of nights of poor sleep because you're anxious	Having trouble sleeping most nights
A small increase in your anxiety symptoms during exam week when you're more stressed and tired	A significant increase in your stress or anxiety level that makes it hard to do many routine things and that isn't responsive to the skills you've used
Little to no difficulty going to school, extracurricular activities, and getting out of the house due to anxiety	Difficulty going to school, extracurricular activities, and getting out of the house due to anxiety

Obviously, you'd rather deal with a pothole than a sinkhole. The best way to ensure that is to plan ahead, so it's time to look into the future.

Skill #1: Looking into Your Crystal Ball

Even though there's no such thing as a crystal ball, there are some aspects of our lives we can forecast with reasonable accuracy. Obviously, there will be some unexpected events you won't be able to predict, like a global pandemic, but there are lots of events you can.

What Can You Expect?

If you live in the Northern Hemisphere, the school year for most students begins sometime between August and September. So, besides knowing when school will start and end, you can also plan for holiday weekends and time off for vacations, as these dates are usually posted well in advance. Student athletes already know which sports are offered in each season and may have access to the practice and game schedules six to twelve months in advance. Another example is learning to drive, which in many countries occurs sometime between ages sixteen and eighteen. If you know you'll be eligible to learn to drive at your next birthday (and this is something you want to do), you can prepare by learning the rules and scheduling any instruction you may need. Can you think of other events or activities that you can expect in the next twelve months? Take a few minutes, and using your journal or your phone, list all the events and activities that you feel fairly confident will be part of your life over this next year.

Why Does It Matter?

It's important to think ahead and predict major events and activities in your life because doing this can help alert you to uncertainty and potential stress or anxiety. Knowing events or activities in advance can also assist you in planning how to cope with changes and uncertainty by using specific skills outlined in this book, and this applies to both positive and negative events. For example, many people feel excited and happy about going on vacation.

However, vacations generate uncertainty and stress as they often require changes to our schedule, possible jet lag, being away from friends, and other demands that are not part of our typical routine. Of course, we are often willing to trade these demands for the benefits that come with being on vacation, but they are demands nonetheless. Looking at your twelve-month forecast list of events, activities, and situations, consider the potential for uncertainty and stress not only with the negative or challenging events but also with the positive ones. Rate each item using a 1, 2, or 3 for your level of stress/anxiety/uncertainty, where 1 = low, 2 = medium, and 3 = high.

Staring Uncertainty in the Face

As you can see, being aware of the pending events you may face doesn't mean you can eradicate uncertainty. Rather, the point is to recognize that when a particular event occurs, it will bring with it some uncertainty that may feel stressful. And when that time approaches, it will become a prompt for you to use the skills you've learned throughout this book to help you get through the situation with less worry, anxiety, and life disruption. So, while you cannot prevent uncertainty, you can prepare for it. Return to the *It's a Wrap* section earlier in this tip, and select one or two skills you can use if uncertainty presents in the next twelve-month forecast of events, activities, and situations described above. Write these skills down next to each event listed. It's okay if you want to use the same skill for more than one event. But before we end this last tip, we want to share with you one more skill to increase your strength and energy as you move forward on your life's path.

Skill #2: Snacks, Naps, and Stretches to Nourish Yourself on Your Journey

If you've gone on a road trip before, you know there are a few essentials you'll need, like gas in the tank, snacks to eat, good music or conversation, and opportunities to stretch. If you go on overnight trips, you may also need a good place to sleep. Your life's journey can be a long-term road trip! And because life is a journey, and not a destination, you'll want to plan some healthy habits to increase your ability to pursue your passions without anxiety and uncertainty sending you off the road into a sinkhole. The following are some general guidelines for healthy living during the adolescent years:

Sleep: Research shows that teenagers should be getting about eight to ten hours of sleep nightly. This can be hard if you have an early start to your day, but it's the goal. In addition, sleeping in on weekends or napping during the day are sleep disrupters that can negatively affect your sleep cycle. Experts recommend establishing a fixed and firm wake time you follow seven days a week to help you fall asleep quicker and get more hours of sleep over time. Also, because a bedtime routine works well to prepare your body for sleep, try winding down screen use about one hour before bed, reading or doing a calming activity thirty minutes before lights out, and going to bed only when you're sleepy. Finally, having a dark, cool, and quiet place to sleep will help you fall asleep faster and improve your overall sleep quality (Harvey 2016; Mullin and Simon 2017).

Nutrition: There's so much information available on the dos and don'ts of healthy eating that it can be confusing to know what's right to do and not do. It all comes back to the oft-repeated rule of *everything in moderation.* This means that all foods are available in reasonable amounts, and that you make smart choices. You don't need us to tell you that a good breakfast doesn't come from a vending machine. The goal is to do your best when you can, even if once in a while your best is pretzels and water from the vending machine! This means aiming for three meals a day and a few snacks in between. Try to balance your meals so you have a healthy balance of vegetables, protein, and grains. Limit caffeine after lunch or early afternoon to help you fall asleep at night. Keep sugary snacks to a minimum, and avoid eating them before bedtime. Your dentist will thank you!

Exercise: North American guidelines recommend that youth ages twelve to seventeen get about one hour of exercise daily (Government of Canada 2019; US Department of Health and Human Services 2018). This might be easy if you're involved in sports or dance, but otherwise might seem staggeringly high. Exercise can be anything that raises your heart rate, which may include dancing to music, walking to school, helping with yard or housework, playing Frisbee, vigorous playing with a dog, walking around a mall, and other creative ideas that get you moving. Exercise not only helps strengthen your heart but also helps metabolize food and improves the quality of your sleep. Try to include some of these activities, if not daily, most days in your week to keep alert and able to cope with stress, anxiety, and uncertainty.

Balance: Because your life is already packed with school demands, chores, and routine stress, it's important to schedule some balance. Balance may come through good sleep, nutrition, and exercise, but it can also come through pleasure and recreation. If 90 percent of your day feels heavy and stress-filled, you're imbalanced. Making sure you have at least a few times each day, or a few days a week, when you can "play" and enjoy yourself will restore your balance. Try looking at your pursuits list in Tip 7 for ideas or consider some of these: music, dance, drawing, painting, books, TV shows, movies, coding, friends, cooking, walks, photography, shopping, eating out, social gatherings, and more.

NOTING YOUR PROGRESS

At the start of this book, we asked you to take a quiz and rate your level of need for certainty. Now that you have read all ten tips, we're asking you to retake the quiz from Tip 1 and notice if there's been any change in your score. The hope is that your score has dropped, which would indicate that you now feel more confident and capable in dealing with uncertainty in your life.

1. When I open my eyes in the morning,

   A. I love to know exactly what the day will look like, mapping out my schedule hour by hour, and feeling ready for everything.

   B. I think about what I have to do, but feel okay if my schedule changes as the day unfolds because I don't have to know the precise order of events.

   C. I prefer to keep all options open, not having a plan and letting the day evolve naturally.

2. I post a reply stating my opinion to a group chat and immediately regret sending it when no one responds for several minutes.

   A. I find sitting with the discomfort of not knowing why no one has replied is almost unbearable. I really need someone to write something now! I feel insecure, and I think about deleting the post so my opinion isn't criticized.

   B. I wonder why no one has replied. Maybe they disagree with me? I think of different ways to respond, but feel okay that it'll get sorted out.

   C. I move on to something else to pass the time. I figure other people are also doing a bunch of stuff while we're texting, and they'll post something eventually. Even if they don't agree with my opinion, it's okay. I love debates.

3. When I'm waiting for my grade on a quiz or test...

   A. It's the worst! It's on my mind constantly and I feel like I'll burst out of my skin if I don't find out soon. I sleep badly and I'm grumpy the next day.

   B. It bugs me, and I want to know how I did, but I can hang in there. No news is good news, right?! It's a little hard to fall asleep, but I do.

   C. Tests and quizzes don't bother me because there's nothing I can do about them now. I can wait as long as it takes. My sleep is good and so is my mood.

4. My friends and I have applied to (fill in the blank: *college/a job/a volunteer position*). We're supposed to hear back today.

   A. Everybody else seems cool with waiting, but I can barely make it through my first class. I'm feeling so overwhelmed. I'm checking my email and social media constantly. What if it's coming via snail mail? Maybe I should head home to intercept the mail.

   B. It's hard to concentrate on school knowing that things will change if I get the response I want. Still, I take a deep breath and remind myself I'll know soon.

   C. As soon as I get to school, I'm so busy with my day, I hardly think about the application.

5. I'm in the middle of class, and I notice a strange lump on my arm.

   A. I immediately think the worst and text my parent to pick me up and take me to the doctor. I can't function. A zillion possibilities fly through my brain, and I can't stop searching for information online, so I know what I have, and whether it can be treated immediately.

   B. Weird. That wasn't there yesterday, was it? I text my parent and ask them to schedule a medical appointment. I figure it's probably nothing and will wait to see the doctor.

   C. Weird. That wasn't there yesterday, was it? I must remember to ask my parent if I should see my doctor.

6. My friends want to hang out this weekend, and we start discussing plans at the end of the school day.

   A. Everybody seems fine deciding things at the last minute, and I hate that I'm not like that. I want us to make a firm and final plan now so I can relax. If I don't find out a few days in advance, I might not go at all.

   B. I'd prefer to make a firm and final plan now, but I get that my friends need to check in with others. It's annoying, but I'll go anyway.

   C. I'm fine with us taking our time. I can wait and play it by ear.

7. My family wants to try a new restaurant instead of going to our usual place.

   A. I immediately go online to view the menu and prepare. I have to know all my options and think carefully about the best thing to order.

   B. I start imagining the kinds of food they might serve and what type of entrée I might like. I hope it's as good as our usual place.

   C. I'm excited to try something new. I love surprises! I was getting bored by our usual place anyway.

8. We just finished our course selection planning, but it'll be another month before we know whether we get our first choice.

   A. A month is an eternity. I just don't think it's biologically possible for me to wait that long. I have to start planning my schedule for next year and prepare for each new teacher.

   B. A month is a long time to wait. I start imagining how it will go if I get my first choice, and if I don't.

   C. A month? A week? A day? It makes no difference because the new school schedule will be what it will be now or in a month from now.

9. I'm about to get a vaccine at school.

   A. I feel afraid of the pain and how I'll manage. Last time was awful, and that scene keeps replaying in my mind. What if I freak out in front of everyone?

   B. I don't like shots, and I'm pretty nervous about how this is gonna go, but I know I'll get through it.

   C. No one likes shots, but I can deal with it. This doesn't really bother me.

10. I heard my parents arguing late last night. They were loud, but I'm not sure what it was all about.

    A. I have to find out what this means. It could be a major crisis like they're gonna get a divorce! Perhaps we've run out of money? Is a family member ill? I'm too scared to ask them, but I will because I need to know so I can prepare.

    B. It sucks when people I care about fight, and it makes me sad. I wish I knew what it was about so I could help them.

    C. It sucks when people I care about fight, but it's not my business. If it concerns me, I'm sure I'll find out soon enough.

What's your score? Tally your responses as follows and add up your final score:

A = 3

B = 2

C = 1

Open to anything (Score = 10–12)

I'm pretty chill not knowing what's coming. Once in a while, I get snagged by a big thing, but otherwise I'm cool with uncertainty.

Life is like a box of chocolates; you never know what you're gonna get.
—Forrest Gump

Middle of the road (Score = 13–22)

I like certainty about the big things, but generally don't sweat the little stuff. I know what's important and needs my time and attention, and what doesn't.

Sometimes I get caught up in the drama of the little things and find I'm anxious, but generally I can figure it out.

Be moderate in order to taste the joys of life in abundance.

—Epicurus

Love my GPS (Score = 23–30)

I need lots of certainty about everything: the big stuff and the little stuff. I get swept up in the unknowns, and this causes such stress and worry in my life. I wish it didn't happen this way, but it does.

Never quit certainty for hope.

—Scottish proverb

WHAT'S THE VERDICT?

Have you noticed a change since you started reading this book? Perhaps your score has dropped, which is cause to celebrate. Yippee! But even if it hasn't changed, or perhaps not as much as you had hoped it would, there may be some explanation for this. Take a look at these reasons why positive changes may not happen at the pace we wish for.

Positive changes take time: Sometimes the positive changes we make take time to register in our brains, so you may want to give it a little more time and then try retaking the quiz in a few weeks or a month.

Positive changes require practice: For some people, a score that hasn't changed much may be a signal that they need to practice more often or with more situations. If this is your case, it might be worth returning to Tips 7 or 8 and asking yourself: *Are my passions obvious to me? Do I have a clear list of pursuits I want to achieve? Am I consistently using GRASP methods?* And finally: *Do I feel confident that I have a core list of skills I can use when anxiety and uncertainty strike?* (Even just two to four skills may be sufficient.)

Positive changes need support: If you believe you have carefully read and applied the skills and ideas in this book and you remain dependent on life being certain to keep your anxiety in check, it might be time to seek help from a mental health professional. Talk with a parent, teacher, school counselor, or other trusted adult who can help you find resources in your area.

TIP 10 TAKEAWAYS

In this tip, you learned the following:

- To help you continue to pursue your passions even with life's inherent uncertainties, the goal is to become comfortable with uncertainty by remembering and implementing the key points and skills from Tips 1–10.

- Even when potholes and sinkholes try to drive you off course, knowing what events to expect over the next twelve months and having a list of your favorite skills to help will make your journey smoother.

- Ensuring you have adequate sleep, good nutrition, exercise, and balance in your daily life will keep you healthy and strong as your journey continues.

This chapter's mission was to help you prepare for the next year and beyond by pulling together all your new knowledge and putting it into action. How prepared do you now feel to apply your new knowledge to live your life fully even when uncertainty shows up?

1	2	3	4	5
A little		*some*		*very much*

Conclusion

We've arrived at the end of this book, but your journey is just beginning. We hope you've gained some useful strategies to help you along the way as you pursue your passions and live a life filled with equal parts of joy, striving, and fulfillment. Although uncertainty will be present and stress, worry, and fear may also show up from time to time (not to mention a host of other challenging emotions such as sadness, anger, and shame), the key is to struggle less and live more. Struggling with uncertainty and getting tricked into believing we need to control everything only takes us off our journey's path. Instead, by using some of your new skills, you can learn to step back from the need for certainty and practice doing things differently than you have done in the past. We've shared a variety of teen stories throughout this book, and we'd like to conclude with one last entry: Sam's story.

Meet Sam

I'm Sam (he/him), and I'm sixteen years old. I've attended five schools in eleven years, so I'm no stranger to change. But, because of all these changes, I've struggled with anxiety about being in new situations and have had frequent panic attacks. The attacks make me feel as though I were losing touch with reality and that something dreadful would happen. For the first few months, I tried many strategies to control the worry and prevent panic attacks, but nothing really worked, and the few ideas that were a little helpful required me to put my sleep, grades, relationships, and even my own mental health in jeopardy.

When we first meet teens like Sam in our practice, we offer them a choice: to keep using the ideas they have, or to try some new strategies outlined in this book and see if these can generate different results. Many are understandably scared to try new strategies, but we always remind them that if their old ways of doing things aren't working, they don't have a lot to lose by trying something new. We did this with Sam, and things started to change for him.

When my therapist pointed out that I was smart and hardworking and yet all my efforts weren't paying off, I agreed to try a different approach. I soon discovered that when I applied skills that helped me drop my struggle, make space for anxiety (and sometimes even see it as a friend), I was able to discover and pursue my passions. By accepting uncertainty, the strangest thing happened—the panic attacks started to lessen. I haven't had a panic attack in several months, but the interesting thing is that I know if I did have another one, it wouldn't be that big a deal. I never thought I would believe that, but it's true!

So, we'd like to pose the same question to you that we did to Sam: *if your old ways of coping aren't giving you the payoff you crave, are you willing to try something new?*

We recognize that adolescence is hard, possibly the hardest time in one's life, because this is what our clients tell us, and because we both remember experiencing this phase! But we also hear stories of deep joy and personal growth and get to share in the expansive creativity of our clients. They also demonstrate great courage and strength by being willing to learn and use many of the same skills outlined in this book, skills that enable them to develop a different relationship with uncertainty. When they have the courage to try new ways of coping, like Sam and many others did, they learn that they are able to treat uncertainty as something to accept but not control, and in doing so, discover they have greater freedom to pursue their passions and be their own boss.

They're no longer pushed about by fear and anxiety and can let uncertainty ebb and flow without it interfering in the ways it once did.

Our hope for you is that you found some guidance and inspiration from the stories we shared and the skills we presented, and that these offer you relief from the burden that comes when we seek constant certainty. We invite you to take charge of your life and to recognize that now is your time to try new things. Today is the beginning, and this journey is yours to discover.

References

2015 U.S. Transgender Survey. https://www.ustranssurvey.org/reports.

Arch, J. J., and J. S. Abramowitz. 2015. "Exposure Therapy for Obsessive-Compulsive Disorder: An Optimizing Inhibitory Learning Approach." *Journal of Obsessive-Compulsive and Related Disorders* 6: 174–82.

Bachmann, M. F., M. O. Mohsen, M. F. Kramer, and M. D. Heath. 2020. "Vaccination Against Allergy: A Paradigm Shift?" *Trends in Molecular Medicine* 26 (4): 357–368.

Bleacher Report. 2017. "Kye Allums: Latest News and Updates on Transgender NCAA Hoops Player." https://bleacherreport.com /articles/508283-kye-allums-get-caught-up-on-story-around -transgender-ncaa-hoops-player.

Bowlby, J. 1977. "The Making and Breaking of Affectional Bonds: I. Aetiology and Psychopathology in the Light of Attachment Theory." *British Journal of Psychiatry* 130 (3): 201–210.

Carleton, R. N. 2016. "Into the Unknown: A Review and Synthesis of Contemporary Models Involving Uncertainty." *Journal of Anxiety Disorders* 39 30–43.

Carleton, R. N., P. J. Norton, and G. J. G. Asmundson. 2007. "Fearing the Unknown: A Short Version of the Intolerance of Uncertainty Scale." *Journal of Anxiety Disorders* 21 (1): 105–117.

Carsley, D., and N. L. Heath. 2018. "Effectiveness of Mindfulness-Based Colouring for Test Anxiety in Adolescents." *School Psychology International.* London: SAGE Publications.

Ciarrochi, J., L. Hayes, and A. Bailey. 2012. *Get Out of Your Mind and into Your Life for Teens: A Guide to Living an Extraordinary Life*. Oakland, CA: Instant Help.

Cornell University. 2021. "What Does the Scholarly Research Say About the Effect of Gender Transition on Transgender Well-being?" *What We Know: The Public Policy Research Portal*. https://whatweknow .inequality.cornell.edu/topics/lgbt-equality/what-does-the-scholarly -research-say-about-the-well-being-of-transgender-people/.

Craske, M., M. Treanor, C. Conway, T. Zbozinek, and B. Vervliet. 2014. "Maximizing Exposure Therapy: An Inhibitory Learning Approach." *Behaviour Research and Therapy*. 58 (310): 10–23.

Emmons, R. A. 2007. *Thanks! How the New Science of Gratitude Can Make You Happier*. Boston: Houghton Mifflin Harcourt.

Emmons, R. A., J. Froh, and R. Rose. 2019. "Gratitude." In *Positive Psychological Assessment: A Handbook of Models and Measures*, edited by Matthew W. Gallagher and Shane J. Lopez. Washington, DC: American Psychological Association.

Emmons, R. A., and M. E. McCullough, eds. 2004. *The Psychology of Gratitude*. New York: Oxford University Press. 317–332.

Fergus, T. A., and R. N. Carleton. 2015. "Intolerance of Uncertainty and Attentional Networks: Unique Associations with Alerting." *Journal of Anxiety Disorders* 41 (September): 59–64.

Government of Canada. 2019. "Physical Activity Tips for Youth (12–17 Years)." 2019. https://www.canada.ca/en/public-health/services/pub lications/healthy-living/physical-activity-tips-youth-12-17-years.html.

Grupe, D. W., and J. B. Nitschke. 2013. "Uncertainty and Anticipation in Anxiety: An Integrated Neurobiological and Psychological Perspective." *Nature Reviews Neuroscience* 14: 488–501.

Hamilton, D. R. 2017. *Five Side Effects of Kindness: This Book Will Make You Feel Better, Be Happier and Live Longer.* London, UK: Hay House.

Harlow, H. F., and R. R. Zimmermann. 1959. "Affectional Responses in the Infant Monkey; Orphaned Baby Monkeys Develop a Strong and Persistent Attachment to Inanimate Surrogate Mothers." *Science* 130: 421–32.

Harris, R. 2008. *The Happiness Trap: How to Stop Struggling and Start Living: A Guide to ACT.* Boston: Trumpeter.

Harris, R. 2019. *ACT Made Simple: An Easy-to-Read Primer on Acceptance and Commitment Therapy.* Oakland, CA: New Harbinger Publications.

Harvey, A. G. 2016. "A Transdiagnostic Intervention for Youth Sleep and Circadian Problems." *Cognitive and Behavioral Practice* 23 (3): 341–55.

Hayes, L. L., and J. Ciarrochi. 2015. *The Thriving Adolescent: Using Acceptance and Commitment Therapy and Positive Psychology to Help Teens Manage Emotions, Achieve Goals, and Build Connection."* Oakland, CA: Context Press.

Hayes, S. C., J. B. Luoma, F. W. Bond, A. Masuda, and J. Lillis. 2006. "Acceptance and Commitment Therapy: Model, Processes and Outcomes." *Behaviour Research and Therapy* 4 (1): 1–25.

LaFreniere, L. S., and M. G. Newman. 2019. "Probabilistic Learning by Positive and Negative Reinforcement in Generalized Anxiety Disorder." *Clinical Psychological Science* 7 (3): 502–515.

Langford, C. P. H., J. Bowsher, J. P. Maloney, and P. P. Lillis. 1997. "Social Support: A Conceptual Analysis." *Journal of Advanced Nursing* 25 (1): 95–100.

Mullin, B. C., and S. L. Simon. 2017. "Managing Insomnia Symptoms Among Adolescents with Anxiety Disorders." *Evidence-Based Practice in Child and Adolescent Mental Health* 2 (3–4): 123–38.

Neff, K. 2003. "Development and Validation of a Scale to Measure Self-Compassion." *Self and Identity*, 2: 223–50.

Neff, K. 2015. "Self-Compassion Break." https://self-compassion.org/exercise-2-self-compassion-break/.

Neff, K. and O. Davidson. 2016. "Self-Compassion: Embracing Suffering with Kindness." In *Mindfulness in Positive Psychology*, edited by I. Ivtzan and T. Lomas. New York: Routledge.

Olympic Channel. 2020. "Vera Wang Talks About Her Olympics Ambitions." https://www.olympicchannel.com/en/stories/news/detail/vera-wang-talks-about-her-olympics-ambitions/.

Robichaud, M., N. Koerner, and M. J. Dugas, M.J. 2019. *Cognitive-Behavioral Treatment for Generalized Anxiety Disorder: From Science to Practice.* New York: Routledge.

Rowland, L., and O. S. Curry. 2019. "A Range of Kindness Activities Boost Happiness." *Journal of Social Psychology* 159 (3): 340–43.

Schumer, L. 2018. "Why Following Your Passions Is Good for You (and How to Get Started)." *New York Times.* October 10, 2018.

Steinmetz, K. 2021. "Elliot Page Is Ready for This Moment." *Time.* https://time.com/5947032/elliot-page/.

Stibel, J. 2017. "Michael Jordan: A Profile in Failure." *CSQ.* https://csq.com/2017/08/michael-jordan-profile-failure/#.YANJ6hNKjLY.

Sullivan, R., R. Perry, A. Sloan, K. Kleinhaus, and N. Burtchen. 2011. "Infant Bonding and Attachment to the Caregiver: Insights from Basic and Clinical Science." *Clinics in Perinatology* 38 (4): 643–55.

The World from PRX. n.d. "10 Transgender Icons Around the World Who Should Be as Famous as Caitlyn Jenner." https://www.pri.org /stories/2015-06-03/10-transgender-icons-around-world-who-should -be-famous-caitlyn-jenner.

Tseng, J., and J. Poppenk, J. 2019. "Brain Meta-State Transitions Demarcate Thoughts Across Task Contexts Exposing the Mental Noise of Trait Neuroticism." *Nature Communications* 11: 3480.

Turner, M. 2021. "Community Issues." https://www.maureeturner.com /community-issues.

Turrell, S., and M. Bell. 2016. *ACT for Adolescents: Treating Teens and Adolescents in Individual and Group Therapy.* Oakland, CA: Context Press.

U.S. Department of Health and Human Services. 2018. *Physical Activity Guidelines for Americans.* 2nd ed. Office of Disease and Prevention and Health Promotion.

Ward, M. 2017. "5 Things You Didn't Know About Oprah Winfrey." *Vogue.* https://www.vogue.com/article/oprah-winfrey-5-things-you-didnt-know.

Wegner, D. M., D. J. Schneider, S. R. Carter, and T. L. White. 1987. "Paradoxical Effects of Thought Suppression." *Journal of Personality and Social Psychology* 53 (1): 5–13.

Whyte, A. 2021. "Failure Is an Option." https://www.linkedin.com/pulse/2014 1209082049-46477532-failure-is-an-option-10-hugely-successful-failures.

Williams, M. T. 2020. *Managing Microaggressions: Addressing Everyday Racism in Therapeutic Spaces.* New York: Oxford University Press.

World Health Organization. 2019. "Mental Health and Substance Use." https://www.who.int/teams/mental-health-and-substance-use/mental -health-in-the-workplace.

Juliana Negreiros, PhD, is a registered psychologist and researcher in British Columbia, Canada; passionate about working with children, youth, and young adults with anxiety, obsessive-compulsive disorder (OCD), and behavioral difficulties using cognitive behavioral therapy (CBT) and acceptance and commitment therapy (ACT) techniques. Negreiros completed a three-year postdoctoral fellowship at the Provincial OCD Program at the BC Children's Hospital, where she led several studies and coauthored a number of academic papers. Negreiros has provided numerous trainings on anxiety nationally and internationally, is a consultant and collaborator with Anxiety Canada, and codeveloped province-wide curriculums for educators to help students manage anxiety in schools.

Katherine Martinez, PsyD, is a registered psychologist in British Columbia, Canada; with more than twenty years of experience in clinical work, training, and research. Martinez uses CBT, ACT, and dialectical behavior therapy (DBT) to assess and treat anxiety, mood, and childhood disorders in children, adolescents, and young adults, as well as provide parent effectiveness training to parents and caregivers. In addition to direct clinical care, Martinez is also a staff writer and contractor for Anxiety Canada, and is a consultant at CBT Connections—an organization that provides evidence-based training for health professionals working for the government and community-funded agencies at the provincial and regional level in both British Columbia and Saskatchewan.

Foreword writer **Sheri L. Turrell, PhD,** is a clinical psychologist who specializes in helping adolescents move toward a life that matters. Over the past ten years, Turrell has coauthored two ACT texts, supervised graduate students and mental health professionals, and facilitated workshops internationally.

More ⏱Instant Help Books for Teens

An Imprint of New Harbinger Publications

THE RESILIENT TEEN
10 Key Skills to Bounce Back from Setbacks and Turn Stress into Success

978-1684035786 / US $17.95

CONQUER NEGATIVE THINKING FOR TEENS
A Workbook to Break the Nine Thought Habits That Are Holding You Back

978-1626258891 / US $17.95

PUT YOUR WORRIES HERE
A Creative Journal for Teens with Anxiety

978-1684032143 / US $17.95

SOCIAL ANXIETY RELIEF FOR TEENS
A Step-by-Step CBT Guide to Feel Confident and Comfortable in Any Situation

978-1684037056 / US $16.95

THE GROWTH MINDSET WORKBOOK FOR TEENS
Say Yes to Challenges, Deal with Difficult Emotions, and Reach Your Full Potential

978-1684035571 / US $18.95

YOUR LIFE, YOUR WAY
Acceptance and Commitment Therapy Skills to Help Teens Manage Emotions and Build Resilience

978-1684034659 / US $17.95